KINETON IN THE GREAT WAR

Bibliography

Among the hundreds of books about the First World War, those I found invaluable were

Norman Holding, *World War I Army Ancestry.* Birmingham : Federation of Family History Societies, 2nd Edition,1992.

Norman Holding, *More Sources of World War I Army Ancestry.* Birmingham : Federation of Family History Societies, 2nd Edition,1991.

Lyn Macdonald, *The Roses of No Mans Land.* London : Joseph,1980.

Michelin 1/200,000 maps, Sheets 51, 52, 53, overprinted showing all cemeteries. Available from Commonwealth War Graves Commission, 2 Marlow Road, Maidenhead, Berkshire, SC6 7DX.

KINETON IN THE GREAT WAR

1914 - 1921

GILLIAN ASHLEY-SMITH

Gill Ashley Smith

Brewin Books

Published by Brewin Books,
Studley Warwickshire B80 7LG. March 1998.

ISBN 1 85858 111 7

A British Library Cataloguing in Publication Data
Catalogue record for this book is available from
The British Library.

Typeset in Caxton Book
and made and printed in Great Britain
by Heron Press, Kings Norton, Birmingham.

Contents

Introduction 1

Part One : The Village Responds

Chapter 1	Immediate Action 1914 5
Chapter 2	Recruitment 16
Chapter 3	Clarendon Hospital 23
Chapter 4	Celebrating Peace 45
Chapter 5	Building the War Memorial 50
Chapter 6	After the War 62

Part Two : Kineton People

Chapter 7	The Soldiers and Sailors of the Village 64
Chapter 8	Kineton Roll of Honour - .85
	Complete List of Servicemen
Chapter 9	The Hospital 127
	Warwickshire Hospitals Data
	List of Staff
Chapter 10	Brief Biographies of some Village Leaders : 132
	The Verney family (including Willoughby de Broke)
	The Fielden family
	The Vicars
	The Schoolmasters
	The Agent
	The Doctor

Index of Names 145

Acknowledgments

I would like to acknowledge the help given to me by the following, and to thank them for their time and interest.

The residents of Kineton, especially

David Beaumont

Derrick Brown

Mary Collett

Mollie Edden

David Fisher

Walter Hartless

Bill Roberts

John Wickham

Arthur Wheildon

Kineton Women's Institute.

Jean Frew and Olive Phipps, relatives of the Askew family.

Margaret Moreton and Peter Trenfield, relatives of the Trenfield family.

Captain Timothy Forster, grandson of Joshua and Dora Fielden.

Mick Palmer, for information about the history of the Warwickshire Hunt.

King Edward VI School, Stratford-upon-Avon.

Warwick School.

Kingswood School, Bath.

Hornton Quarries, Ltd.

Brian Johnson of the Warwickshire Yeomanry.

Brigadier J K Chater of the Royal Regiment of Fusiliers.

Major D S Evans of the Liverpool Scottish Museum Trust.

The British Red Cross Museum and Archives.

The Commonwealth War Graves Commission, for much help, and for allowing me to specify the position of the graves of Kineton men

The staff of the Warwickshire County Record Office.

The Shakespeare Birthplace Trust, and the staff of the Record Office.

The Vicar of Kineton, the Rev Charmaine Host, for allowing me to reproduce several photographs of material held at St Peter's Church, and in the parish deposit at the WCRO.

Finally, Dr Sara Serpell, for her most valuable help and advice in making this book readable.

And the one person without whom this book would never been finished - Peter, my husband, for being my companion in finding the graves of the Kineton servicemen in France and Belgium, my encouragement when progress was difficult, my photographer, my editor, my researcher and my support.

List of Illustrations

The War Memorial, 1997 1
The Rolls of Honour 2
A page from the Album of photographs. 4
Middle School, Warwick Road, about 1910. 6
Dora Fielden. 8
The Golf Hotel, Le Tréport. 9
Members of the Home Defence Group, soon after their formation. 11
Warwickshire Hunt Kennels, 1997 17
Stable lads at the kennels, about 1914. 18
Harry Wisdom 20
A certificate from the first training course in Farnborough. 23
Clarendon House Hospital. 25
Nurses and patients on the steps of Clarendon House Hospital. 26
Walton House, the first extension to the hospital accommodation. 27
Kineton House 28
A Ward, Clarendon House Hospital 29
Lady Willoughby de Broke 31
A Red Cross certificate. 33
Mrs Mary Baldwin. 34
A Bruce Bairnsfather cartoon. 37
The funeral cortege of Corporal Thomas. 40
Queen Alexandra's certificate. 42
A Peace greetings card 46
A membership certificate of the Comrades of the Great War. 48
The site of the War Memorial, before it was built. 51
Brigstock Market Cross and Kineton War Memorial compared. 53
The arms at the top of the memorial. 54
The inscriptions 56
The programme for the Dedication Ceremony 59
The Unveiling, Sunday July 10, 1921 60
W H B Yerburgh, in his naval uniform. .65
The grave of J E W Collett at Prowse Point Cemetery 69
W H Hutton. 72
The Trenfield family. 73
A communication from the front 75

Horace Askew. 77
William Barnes in the Stratford Police Force. 78
Percy Fisher. 80
Raymond Fisher 81
The grave of Douglas Smith 83
George Baldwin in naval uniform 86
John Coleman 87
The grave of John Coleman, as it was first marked, and today 87
Geoffrey Hartless, and his medals. 91
Charles Hudson 92
George Plummer. 95
The memorial card for Denis Rouse. 96
Richard Greville Verney, 19th Lord Willoughby de Broke 133
Joshua Fielden. 136
Hugh Holbech 139
Arthur Watson 140
Leonard Goodenough 141
Joseph Chandler. 143

Photo credits

Ownership of the photographs is as follows.
David Beaumont 37, 40, 46, 53, 60
Derrick Brown 48
Mary Collett 87
Mollie Edden 23, 33, 34, 42
David Fisher 80, 81
Walter Hartless 75, 91
Margaret Moreton 73
Gwen Rawlins 18
Arthur Wheildon 11, 96
British Red Cross Museum and Archives 9
Kineton Women's Institute 8
Kineton and District Local History Group 6, 28, 51, 143
Stratford Birthplace Trust 78
Warwickshire County Record Office . .4, 20, 25, 26, 29, 72, 77, 91, 92, 95
The remaining illustrations are from the author's collection.

Introduction

Almost every town and village in Britain and France has a War Memorial. Most of these monuments were erected soon after the end of the First World War, in recognition of the courage of those who had given their lives for their country, and in the hope and belief that no such sacrifice would ever be needed again. As the years pass fewer and fewer people can recall the faces of those whose names are recorded, and it has become the duty of the local historian to make a record of what these men did and how the ordinary people of town and country responded to the call of war, before the limit of living memory is reached.

Kineton, Warwickshire, is an old market town which lies between Stratford-upon-Avon, Warwick and Banbury, almost exactly 11 miles from each. It is now of lesser importance than formerly, called a 'village' by its 2000 inhabitants, and has at its centre a stone war memorial which names the thirty-eight Kineton men who died between the years 1914 and 1919 as a direct result of the First World War. It gives only their names and ranks - regiments and dates of death are omitted.

The War Memorial, 1997

1

So it was in 1995 that I started to search the corners of the village church in the hope that some record of the detail missing from the war memorial could be found. I came upon two framed Rolls of Honour, recording the names of all those who had served. Still no details were given, but it was at this point, the finding of the two Rolls of Honour in a dusty corner at the back of the church, that my personal interest in the story of Kineton in the Great War came alive - for these Rolls of Honour had been 'amended'. The original scrolls, purchased from Mowbray's, had been carefully cut and pasted, and the entries re-arranged in alphabetical order, thus successfully concealing the information I had hoped to gain about the time at which men had gone to the forces. Despite the fulsome thanks recorded in the Parish Magazine, perhaps this re-writing had not been a good idea!

We thank the Rev Guernsey Walsingham Webb for his kindness in rewriting the list of those from this parish who served in the Great War. He has done the work with his well-known artistic skill, and we are grateful for this service. The two frames containing the list now hang in the church [1].

There are also bills and receipts for the cost of framing and fixing the Rolls in oak and under glass - 11s 0d and 9s 6d for fixings.[2]

The Rolls of Honour, which were 'amended' after the war

The existence of the Rolls was described in the Parish Magazine. It revealed that the first Roll was given by Mrs Ellick, who gave it "to be hung in the church in perpetuity in memory of her son Charlie"[3]. There is an additional note that she presented a second one in August 1916, as the first was full, confirmation of the rate at which young men were leaving the village. Enquiries in the village of today failed to reveal any knowledge at all of the Ellick family. The fact that the name had originally been quoted in the parish magazine as Elliot, and later corrected, made me think that the man and his mother might not have been 'local'. Even more noticeably in the re-writing, the name of this son, Charlie, had mysteriously changed from "C. M. M. Ellick" (as on the War Memorial) to "C. Ellick MM", with its implication of a military medal.

The lack of any idea into which regiments the men went, or when, was to be a considerable problem in finding out about their experiences in the War, but one other unusual source of evidence came to light. The Parish Magazine of December 1917 stated that

The vicar and churchwardens have accepted a handsomely bound volume to contain photos of men who have joined HM forces from our parish. Presented by Captain W H Hutton, MC MFA, it bears on its roan bound cover in gilt lettering "Kineton Roll of Honour". Photos should be sent to the Vicar's Warden (Mr G W Webb)[4]

The Stratford Herald expanded a little on the presentation and how it was planned to display the volume, and reported that "the vicar remarked that it would be greatly valued, and passed down for many years."[5] The book was found in an unopened box at the County Record Office in May 1995, and was then complete with a very dilapidated cover exactly as described. It is now properly conserved and available at DR 746/29.

The book contains the portraits, names and a brief service history of 46 servicemen, with two portraits of one, and three unnamed men, a total of 50 photographs. Eight of them lost their life, and are named on the War Memorial.

Eventually, by reading the Stratford Herald, from parish and school magazines, and by talking to the oldest residents of Kineton, it has been possible to piece together the following story - the story of 'The Great War' at home and abroad.

Pte George Edgar Askew.
King's Royal Rifles.
Joined up Dec.1914.
Killed in France.
July 30. 1915.
Aged 24 years.

Pte Oliver Joseph Askew
Royal Warwick Regt
Joined up July 1917.
Killed in France
March 1918
Aged 25 years.

Pte Frederick Askew
Machine Gun Corps
Joined up Aug 1916
Demobilised April 1919.

A page from the Album of photographs. This page shows three of the four Askew brothers, of whom only one survived.

1 *Parish Magazine of Burton Dassett et al (Parish Magazine)* September 1923
2 Churchwarden's Accounts and Vouchers, at Warwickshire County Record Office (WRCO) DR 212
3 *Parish Magazine*, November 1915
4 ibid., December 1917
5 *Stratford upon Avon Herald*, 5 April 1918

PART ONE - The Village Responds

Chapter One
Immediate Action, 1914

Outbreak of War

When Britain declared war on Germany on 4th August, 1914, Kineton was caught up in the war effort very rapidly. The Territorials left Kineton railway station on the midday trains on Wednesday and Thursday, 5th and 6th August; on Friday 7th August the Stratford Herald reported that "the war authorities are scouring the district for horses" and by 14th August the Red Cross announced that many homes were open to receive the wounded if necessary.[1] There were even offers[2] of the larger premises as temporary hospitals. Mrs Brand offered to put 30 beds at the Manor House in Manor Lane (now run as a nursing home); Mrs Fielden was prepared to have 12 beds at her home, Kineton House, which has now been converted to the 'Mansion House' private apartments at Little Kineton; Mrs Gaskell at Diana Lodge, Little Kineton, Mrs Dalgety at Woodley House, Warwick Road (now Haven House Rest Home), and Mr Webb at the Middle School thought they could each manage 10 beds; and the Church Rooms, Southam Street (now private housing) was thought to be suitable for 20.

In fact, the first mobilisation of Voluntary Aid Detachment hospitals in England was made on 15th October - and Clarendon House, Bridge Street, Kineton (not included in that first list above) was part of the first wave. It received its first wounded on 20th November 1914. The part played by Kineton in that initiative is the subject of Chapter Three.

Hospitality for the Belgians

Certainly by the middle of October it had become apparent that practical help would indeed be needed. The German refusal to honour the neutrality

Middle School, Warwick Road, about 1910. The man outside is headmaster Mr G W Webb

of Belgium in the hostilities had been a major cause of Britain's involvement in the war, and as the Germans swung in a great arc of fighting towards France, Belgium, with its small army, was overrun. Two Kineton ladies, the Misses Hunter and Whately of Warwick Road, both school health inspectors, called a meeting to discuss the possibility of offering hospitality to Belgian refugees. It was decided that, if a suitable house could be found in the village, they should aim to provide for a family of poorer Belgians. The district was to be canvassed for gifts of clothes and food such as jams, apples, onions, potatoes, carrots and turnips, which would be sent to headquarters if no house were found[3]. There is no record of Belgians arriving, though there is a brief reference to Belgian refugees celebrating mass at the home of Mr F G Sumner, a prominent Roman Catholic, who lived at Dene House, Bridge Street[4]. Certainly money was raised for the refugees, including £8 10s 0d from the church collection on 6th January 1915[5].

Working Parties

Even before this, in August 1914, Mrs Dora Fielden, wife of the Joint Master of the Warwickshire Hunt, set up a working party at her home,

Kineton House, to make clothes and necessities for the soldiers. She herself provided the materials, and there was a ready response, with people coming from 5pm to 7pm every evening. On 13th November 1914 the following items were ready for distribution.

92 shirts	85 prs socks	6 Red Cross dresses
36 collars	27 night-shirts	21 Red Cross aprons
16 nightingales	23 prs bed socks	54 prs Red Cross sleeves
9 helmets	10 bed jackets	12 pillows
12 mufflers		

Some items were kept for use by the VAD, and the rest were sent to the companies led by some of the well known village servicemen - to Dora Fielden's nephew, Captain Anthony Fielden of the 10th Hussars; to Lord Willoughby de Broke's son, Second Lieutenant John Peyto Verney in the 4th Dragoons, and to Lord Willoughby's nephew Captain Oswald Tritton[6].

A Hospital in France

Mrs Fielden was also quickly involved by influential Kineton friends in raising money to set up a hospital for the wounded in Le Tréport, France. Mrs Brand, of the Manor House, a distant relation by marriage to the Fielden family, was instrumental in the setting up of this hospital, with her friend the Hon Lady Murray.

The scheme has been approved by the Directeur du Service de Santé at Rouen, and a suitable building has been provided by the French Government, who will also make certain allowances towards the maintenance of the institution. It is intended to treat indiscriminately the wounded soldiers of all the Allied Forces. The medical arrangements are under the direction of Mr S Osborn FRCS who has had a large experience of this kind in the South African War, the Balkan War, and the present war. The building, which will accommodate fifty to sixty patients, stands high above the sea, and is provided with water, heating, electric light and baths. The cost of maintenance is estimated at £250 per month, and a sum of about £1300 is required for the initial expenditure on equipment, stores etc. Contributions are requested towards either of these branches of expenditure.[7]

By February 1915 the Stratford Herald was able to report that sufficient

Dora Fielden

NOUVELLE CRÉATION

AUX "TERRASSES"

par le TRÉPORT-MERS   *(Seine-Inférieure)*

—❯ GOLF HOTEL ❮—

OUVERT TOUTE L'ANNÉE

Même Direction que le TRIANON HOTEL   A. STEINER, DIRECTEUR

The Golf Hotel, Le Tréport. (Photograph by kind permission of The British Red Cross Museum and Archives)

funds had been raised, and that "all the staff give their services free (a surgeon, two dressers, three nurses and three wardmaids)"[8]

In fact all 63 beds were full from 12th December 1914, and by 7th June 1916, with the aid of a grant from the Red Cross, it became the No 10 Red Cross Hospital, Le Tréport - a hospital for British officers, specialising in fractured femur cases[9]. Originally called the Anglo-French hospital, it was housed in the 'Golf Hotel' and from 1st December 1914, received wounded from the fighting line at Arras, Souchez, Neuville St Vaast, and Notre Dame de Lorette[10]. Throughout the war Lady Murray remained responsible for the maintenance of the hospital, and Mrs Brand spent several months of the year helping at it.

Women's Role

The idea of women nursing and making clothes was traditional, but as the war dragged on, women became more and more essential to the economy, and more and more involved in things which had until then been seen as a male prerogative. Kineton was at the centre of the campaign for introducing female labour onto the land. The campaign was inaugurated in South West Warwickshire at a meeting held in Kineton on Tuesday, 6th June 1916, and organised by Mrs A D Flower, mayoress of Stratford-upon-Avon. The Church rooms were packed, and Joshua Fielden, (Joint Master of the Hunt, and husband of Dora Fielden, who was involved with the running of the voluntary hospital), introduced the speakers.

The first was Mrs Hobbs, of Kelmscott, Oxfordshire, the wife of a prominent agriculturist. She exhorted farmers to keep up the food supply in as successful a way as the Germans, using women's labour if necessary. "Any woman," said Mrs Hobbs, using a quotation from Gulliver's Travels[11] to illustrate her point, "who 'helps to make two blades of corn grow where one grew before', is doing as much as the man fighting in the trenches or the woman making munitions." If there were women not physically fit enough to work on the land, then she suggested that they could look after the children of able-bodied women.

The second speaker was Miss Day. She made it clear that those in authority wanted some 400,000 women to come forward, and that her presence at this meeting was to make " these beautiful rural districts" aware of the War. "Working on the land is no picnic", and she hoped the women would put their backs into the work and realise that it was a job to go on with. "Every woman in receipt of separation allowances with no children to look after should certainly respond to the call".

The third speaker, Mr Allsebrook of the Board of Agriculture, gave some detailed facts and figures about agricultural production, and explained that between 250,000 and 300,000 men formerly connected with agriculture had gone into the ranks of the Army and Navy - hence the need for women to farm. He continued (to much laughter)

One farmer delivered himself as follows - 'Women ain't no good; never was and never will be' - but afterwards he learnt that this sportsman had been married three times.

But he was able to promise a short course of instruction for the volunteers, which would at least prepare them for hoeing and milking, and for general farm duties.

Support and thanks were expressed in all ways, not least by some twelve members of the audience indicating their willingness to try land work.[12]

Home Defence

The older men, meanwhile, had organised themselves into a 'home defence' committee, started by[13]

J Fielden   Mr Hutton, Agent to Lord Willoughby

Dr Oldmeadow, a village G P	ex Inspector Smith
Mr Ashford	E Coles
Mr Sutcliffe	F Griffin
A Griffin	J Chandler, headmaster of the National School

By December 1914 there were 60-70 members. They were drilled until 1916 by Sergeant Coles of Southam, with Joshua Fielden as commandant and Colonel Basil Hanbury, Lord Willoughby de Broke's brother-in-law, as the nominal vice lieutenant, though he was away on military duty.[14]

The "Volunteer Training Corps" as they were soon called, met regularly and were supported enthusiastically. Mr Fielden asked to use the Church rooms, where they often met, as a Rifle Range[15], and presumably enthusiasm was such that a shooting competition was organised by Mr F S Sumner the following summer.

Members of the Home Defence Group, soon after their formation.

The final round took place in very unsettled weather; nevertheless quite a large number assembled to witness it. There was an interval for tea when Mrs Sumner entertained all those interested in the corps. The competitors and also the wounded soldiers' tea was provided by Mrs Ed(d)en in the pavilion.* Among those present were, besides the host and hostess, Lady Willoughby de Broke, Colonel and Mrs Hanbury, Mrs Fielden, Miss Perry, the Rev and Miss Yerburgh, Mr Lakin, Mrs Pierson-Webber, the Rev A H Watson and others.[16]

Four of the five prize winners at the competition were men who would be serving in the forces before the end of the war. Of them, the winner, Harry W Freeman, and one of the runners-up, Frederick Hancock, had already enlisted and were waiting for orders for active service; another runner-up, W Bretherick, was to have a distinguished career in the Navy; and the fourth, Geoffrey Bancroft, was only twenty and studying for pharmaceutical qualifications. All three of the winners of the boys' competition which followed the men's also went to fight when they were old enough, and all returned.

* The wounded soldiers came from Clarendon hospital, which was by then fully operational, and the pavilion was at the top of the Warwick road, on the site of the present Station Garage.

Billeted Troops

Yet another major demand was made on the people of Kineton within a few months of the outbreak of war, and in many ways it must have been the most spectacular. In January 1915, it was announced that 250 soldiers were to be billeted in Kineton.

On Saturday afternoon, 6th February 1915, seven officers and 232 men of the West Riding Territorial Royal Engineers duly arrived by special train at Kineton station. The Stratford Herald had nothing but praise for the efforts made in Kineton for their comfort:

They are billeted generally in private houses and are made heartily welcome. The Church rooms are thrown open from 5pm - 9pm daily and five to seven newspapers, and writing material and games are provided for the use of the boys. From 7pm - 9pm a smoking concert takes place. The executive committee is
Lady Willoughby de Broke, wife of the Lord of the manor
The Hon Mabel Verney, Lord Willoughby's aunt

Mrs Fielden
Miss Heath Stubbs
Miss Yerburgh, the Vicar's sister
and the working committee consists of sidesmen and choirmen. Mr Webb is Hon Sec and managing director of the concert. The Wesleyans have also thrown open their schoolroom for reading etc. for the soldiers.[17]

The Parish Magazine for April 1915 is more specific about the financial commitment needed for the undertaking. "The principal London and Birmingham morning papers, as well as the *Graphic, Sphere, Punch* and other weeklies" were provided, and the soldiers used "50 quires of writing paper and 1000 envelopes provided for them by Mrs Fielden, Mr Webb and Mr E Parke." Miss Yerburgh lent a piano, and Mrs Fielden a gramophone and records. The organisers also met the cost of cleaning and loss of income when the County Council classes had to be relocated.

Entertaining the Troops

One of the concerts organised for the entertainment of the visiting soldiers is reported in full in the Stratford Herald.

On Thursday evening of last week a very interesting programme was arranged including songs, recitations and a play, to entertain the soldiers in the Church rooms, and a very enjoyable time it proved. The proceedings commenced with a pianoforte duet by Mr and Miss Webb, an overture from 'Faust'; Mr Sidney Wheildon sang 'Glorious Devon'; Mrs Hanbury gave a recitation 'Victoria Cross', which was received with rapt attention, and Mr Clifton also sang. A dialogue followed, entitled 'Miss Civilisation'. Mr H B Verney as Hatch, Mr G W Webb as Reddy, and Mr Heath-Stubbs as Harry, made three most ferocious looking burglars. Alice (Miss Civilisation), the daughter of a rich railway owner, was cleverly and sweetly personified by Miss Clare Verney. Alice's invalided mother, who was heard and not seen, was represented by Miss Maude Webb. The police inspector who captured the burglars in making off with their booty, was taken by Mr Chandler. Mr R Verney arranged the limelights which greatly added to the realism of the whole proceedings, and the National Anthem brought a very pleasant time to a close.[18]

It is quite possible that this particular concert had its roots in one of the Verney houseparties held at the rectory in Lighthorne, but even so, that such a concert could be devised and put on only four weeks after the soldiers arrived in the village, shows not only how normal was the idea of 'home grown' entertainment at this time, but also how warmly Kineton society welcomed its visitors.

Visiting Troops Depart

There are various brief reports of minor injuries sustained during training being treated at Clarendon hospital, but the troops' stay in Kineton seems largely uneventful, until the spectacle presented just before they left.

Monday last was an important day with 2nd battalion Hampshire Regiment, who mustered at full strength with transport wagons and field kitchens, and in marching order proceeded by way of Wellesbourne and Kineton to Radway Grounds. They were under the command of Lt-Colonel Carrington-Smith and a full complement of officers. At the foot of the Edgehills they were joined by 1st Essex and 4th Worcester Regiment, from Banbury, and the West Riding Field Company of Engineers (Territorials) from Kineton. It was typical March weather, cold, with alternating showers of rain and sleet, but the spectacle of so many military men grouped together was a fine one. Brigadier General Napier inspected the Brigade and, we believe, expressed his pleasure at seeing the men so fit. The proceedings were watched by a large company.[19]

They left finally in the middle of March, with cheers from the soldiers for the people of Kineton, and gifts of cigarettes from the villagers for the soldiers. No doubt there were some broken hearts as well - there are several references in the Kineton column of the Stratford Herald to those soldiers of the West Riding who were later killed or wounded in battle.

1   *Stratford upon Avon Herald*, 14 August 1914
2   *Warwick Advertiser*, 15 August 1914
3   *Parish Magazine of Burton Dassett et al. (Parish magazine)* October 1914, and *Stratford upon Avon Herald*, 16 October 1914
4   *Stratford upon Avon Herald*, 17 June 1927
5   Warwick County Record Office, DR 212/37
6   *Stratford upon Avon Herald*, 13 November 1914
7   ibid., 4 December 1914
8   ibid., 26 February 1915

9   Reports of the Joint War Committee, British Red Cross Society and Order of St John, p 346

10 **Binyon, Laurence**. *For Dauntless France*, 1918, p 138

11 **Swift, Jonathan**. *Gulliver's Travels*, Part 2, Chapter 7.

12 *Stratford upon Avon Herald*, 9 June 1916

13 ibid., 20 November 1914

14 ibid., 12 November 1915

15 *Parish Magazine*, January 1915

16 *Stratford upon Avon Herald*, 20 August 1915

17 ibid., 12 February 1915

18 ibid., 5 March 1915

19 ibid., 5 March 1915

Chapter Two
Recruitment

Economic effects

It has been estimated that in the First World War deaths in the country as a whole attributable to the conflict were nearly nine per cent of the male population aged between twenty-five and forty. This figure is fairly accurately represented by the 38 names of Kineton men on the War Memorial. (496 men are recorded by the census in 1911, and 9% of that number is 44.)

Other estimates suggest that about eleven per cent of the total population of the United Kingdom was in uniform for at least some time during the War. On this basis, Kineton, with a population of 1018 (1911 census), would be expected to send 112 of its people to fight. In fact over 250 men from the village, double the expected number, served for at least some of the period 1914-1919, and, it could be argued, this number should be augmented by the 200-plus women of the area who were 'in uniform' serving in the VAD hospital in the village.

Reasons for these discrepancies are perhaps a matter for a professional historian, but it is possible that some suggestions can be made. Kineton is a largely agricultural village and at the time of the Great War the whole country was suffering from agricultural depression. It may be that the lowness of labourers' wages made the prospect of Army pay very attractive. The Kineton economy must also have been closely allied to the fortunes of the Warwickshire Hunt, for a great many of its inhabitants were in service to those who took houses for the hunting season or were engaged in work with the horses. While the figures are obviously not complete, Spennell's Directory for 1914 gives an indication of village employment. It shows

35 farmers and agricultural labourers
11 food suppliers (grocers, fishmongers etc)
7   gardeners
2   butlers
16 clothes suppliers (drapers, dressmakers and laundresses)
25 looking after horses (grooms, blacksmiths etc)

Warwickshire Hunt Kennels, 1997

In addition, the Warwickshire Hunt had been going through a bad time between 1910 and 1913. There was dissatisfaction that the pack was only being hunted twice a week and in February 1909 Lord Willoughby de Broke announced that he was no longer able to pour money into supporting the pack, nor had he the time nor health to devote to being Huntsman. By March 1910 subscriptions (which were the major way in which a hunt pack was supported) had fallen by 72, and the Hunt was almost bankrupt. By the 1911/1912 season an attempt had been made to solve the problems, and Joshua Fielden had offered to come as joint Master of Foxhounds, with a massive injection of enthusiasm and capital which allowed for hunting five days a week. It was agreed to sell all the horses in May 1911 and take the opportunity to improve the quality of the hunting horses, and in December 1912 the hunt supporters noted that "Joshua Fielden and his wife were both set on the best." Nevertheless with only one season between then and the outbreak of War in August 1914, prospects of employment connected with the hunting world of Kineton may still have felt a little shaky, and when the first war entry in the Stratford Herald reads "War authorities are scouring the district for horses"[1] and a few days later,

Kineton in the Great War

Kineton is suffering terribly from the effects of the war in the departure of men and horses. A depot was formed at the kennels, 110 horses being sent away, fifteen of which were from the kennels.[2]

Stable lads at the kennels, about 1914.

then the prospect of life in Kineton must have seemed bleak.

There is little doubt that in the almost feudal set-up of a village which was devoted to serving the upper sections of society, a very high regard was given to patriotism and service of the country, and the village gentry seem to have encouraged this. Joshua Fielden certainly did nothing to hinder his employees who wished to volunteer.

On Tuesday morning, 25th August, the whole of the stablemen from the Kennels, numbering sixteen, left by the 8.20 train en route for Scarborough, there to undergo a medical test. The men all volunteered for cavalry service. Mr and Mrs Fielden were at the station to see the men off, and for their willingness to serve King and Country Mr Fielden gave to each man £2 as a parting gift. He is paying all expenses, and if they do not pass will pay their return journey. He will welcome the others back after the war. The whole of the kennel staff now consists of married men. The men had a good send off both

18

by the 'girls they left behind them' and their many well-wishers and friends. Loud cheers were given as the train steamed out of the station.[3]

In fact "all the men passed but one, and he was too young."[4]

Recruiting drives

Recruiting drives were a feature of the early months of the war.

In mid September the Rugby recruiting rally came to the Green in Kineton, at which the Vicar reported that 40 men had already gone - and that he hoped more would follow. It was also reported that

A reserve regiment of Yeomanry is being formed. Farriers and motor cyclists are wanted, also cooks. Lord Willoughby de Broke will command the squadron [5]

In December 1914, some 200 were present at a meeting in the school, to hear an impassioned appeal for volunteers. "More men are required as it is impossible to cope with odds of ten to one. Man for man our men are far superior to the Germans" said Dr Oldmeadow, the general practitioner in the village, "and country men nearly always make the best soldiers. They are more hardy, and used to discomforts". He even appealed for the women to help by persuading the men to go. Despite its passion, the meeting seems not to have stirred many of the men of Kineton:

A boy, whom Kineton ought to be proud of, was the only one who responded, namely Harry Wisdom, who left home on Monday. Another boy from Butlers Marston offered his services later.[6]

In March 1915 the Royal Warwickshire's band played for an hour in the village as part of a recruiting drive for Kitchener's Army, though we are not told whether it had any more effect than the speeches of three months earlier, but in November 1915 a slightly sterner tone appears, which seems to have produced the intended result:

There are 80 men, married and single, under 40 in the neighbourhood, and it is hoped all single men will come forward now it is clear that they will all be needed.[7]

The Herald was able to report just four weeks later that between seventy and eighty more recruits had been signed up, though this may have had as much to do with the rumours of the coming conscription as with high ideals.

From the Roll of Honour read out in Kineton Church at the beginning of

Harry Wisdom - 'The boy to be proud of'

1916, together with the estimate given above, it would appear that about 195 men of Kineton and the closely neighbouring villages were in the forces by the end of 1915.

Conscription and tribunals

Lord Derby's scheme for conscription was introduced in January 1916, with provision for exemption of some men, mostly those who had already been turned down; those whose work was deemed to be in the national interest; and those upon which a household depended, for example where there was only one man, or where only one son was left after three or four other sons had already been killed or disabled. Men in these categories were able to obtain an exemption certificate if their case was upheld by one of the tribunals set up on a local basis. Kineton's tribunal was that of the Stratford Rural District, and was headed by several of the well-known village men and women, not least Joshua Fielden and the Hon Mabel Verney. As the slaughter at the front lines continued, the age of men called up was raised, with the result that men with large dependent families who felt they were needed at home were being called away to fight. It is not therefore surprising that there was unrest when people thought the rules were being applied unfairly, be it by Government or local tribunal. A meeting of protest was held in Kineton on Thursday 16th March 1916.

A meeting of married men was held at the Public Hall on Thursday evening in last week. Mr F G Sumner presided, and said that the pledge had not been kept to married men. Mr G Freeman [the manager of the Gas Works] moved the following resolutions:-
1) That this mass meeting of married men strongly protests against the calling up of groups for service until the Prime Minister's pledge to married men has been fulfilled in the spirit as well as in the letter, by withdrawing and sending into the services all single men from reserved occupations; starred men in government and public offices, doing work which could be equally well done by women and married men whose family and financial obligations demand that they should have the preference for this class of work; and by stringent revision of the cases of single men exempted by the Tribunals, or rejected as medically unfit, who are in many cases well-known to be perfectly eligible and fit for military service.
2) That the Government must make adequate provision for the financial responsibilities of married attested men before requiring them to serve.

3) That the mobilisation of the married shall be suspended for 28 days until these just demands are dealt with.

He said that he was one of those who canvassed the eligible men, and quite thought the pledge would be carried out. Ways and means had been found for many single men to shirk their responsibilities. Lord Derby, he thought, should resign, and show the Government he was not a party to the non-carrying out of his undertaking.

Various other men spoke in support, including Mr Clifton, Mr Grimes, Mr Trenfield and Mr A Griffin. The resolutions were carried unanimously.[8]

Whether a certain amount of favouritism could be ascribed to these local tribunals is a matter for conjecture, but certainly those sitting on them had a powerful chance to plead for exemption of their own staff.

Of the 50 Kineton men who appeared before the tribunal, only seven were actually refused an exemption certificate, but eighteen of them eventually went into the forces - fear of the 'white feather of cowardice' and pressure from their friends and workmates may have played a part. Joshua Fielden supported successful claims for seven of his employees, though three of them eventually chose to go into the army; Lord Willoughby de Broke supported the claim for six, two of whom were refused exemption.

Decisions made by the local tribunals could still be overruled by appeal. The military representative for the area was given the right to question a decision and send it to appeal court, as was the man involved. As more and more categories of men were called up, and previous grounds for exemption were deemed invalid, re-application for exemption became necessary. All the appeal papers are available in Warwickshire County Record Office at CR 1520, and considerable use has been made of them in drawing up the Roll of Honour in Part Two.

1   *Stratford upon Avon Herald*, 7th August 1914
2   ibid., 28 August 1914
3   ibid., 28 August 1914
4   *Warwick Advertiser*, 29 August 1914
5   *Stratford upon Avon Herald*, 18 September 1914
6   ibid., 4 December 1914
7   ibid., 19 November 1915
8   ibid., 24 March 1916

Chapter Three
Clarendon Hospital

Establishing the Hospital

In 1909, Voluntary Aid Detachments were established by the War Office to fill the gap which existed in the medical organisation of the Territorial Force. Lady Willoughby de Broke, a Vice-President of the British Red Cross Society, was very interested in the scheme, and determined to set up a detachment in Kineton as soon as possible. Under her guidance, 15 Kineton men and 20 women gave in their names as being interested at the outset - in December 1909. By February 1910 a course of lectures was held to enable them to gain the certificate of efficiency from the St John's Ambulance Association, a necessary first step to becoming a 'VAD' member.[1]

One of the certificates from the first training course in Farnborough, Warwickshire.

Further training courses followed, and on October 15, 1910, the Kineton Voluntary Aid Detachment held its first field day.

Red Cross Society - On October 15th the members of the Voluntary aid Detachment in connection with this Society met together for the first time to hold a field day, and made an excellent start with their work. The boy scouts having fought a battle left their wounded lying about the fields near Little Kineton. On news of this being brought to the hospital headquarters at Kineton House, the men of the detachment sallied out in sections, provided with bandages, and extemporised stretchers, to render first aid and to bring in the wounded. In this work they were assisted by two carts. The wounded were in due time all brought in to the receiving station, when Dr Oldmeadow inspected them and criticised the bandaging, etc., they were then passed on to Kineton House. Here a most efficient hospital of 20 beds had been prepared by the ladies of the detachment, who rendered further necessary aid to the patients; the latter were finally inspected thoroughly by Dr Oldmeadow. A field day like this serves to show up just what points there are in the organisation or training, and should lead to even greater efficiency on the next occasion. We understand that our detachment is the first in the County to hold such a field day. The members must see to it that by further advance in their work they continue to hold the first place. It is especially desirable that the sections of the men's detachment should get together from time to time to practise stretcher drill.[2]

Kineton's training and preparation was put to a real and immediate test as soon as war broke out. The capabilities of the Warwickshire County organisation had been tested sporadically, and included the fitting-up of private houses as temporary hospitals,[3] so that, when war broke out, hospitals could be established quickly. In fact Clarendon House, Bridge Street, the tall house opposite the end of Manor Lane, was among the first five VAD hospitals in the county. Lent by Mr J Thursby-Pelham, it had twenty beds and opened on November 18th, 1914[4].

As the war dragged on and casualties on every front exceeded everyone's worst nightmares, the demand for nursing care became even greater and hospitals opened rapidly. In Warwickshire there were thirteen at the end of 1915, twenty-four at the end of 1916, and thirty-five in 1917 (for details see Part Two). The number of beds in Kineton grew from twenty in 1914 to 104 in 1917, by which time the establishment at Clarendon House had expanded to include two further properties. It is interesting to note that the number of beds at the hospital was surpassed only by the hospitals in Solihull, Stratford-on-Avon and Warwick itself, and that Kineton, a tiny community in

Clarendon House Hospital.

comparison, made a contribution out of all proportion to its size.

Because no hospital in Warwickshire was big enough, at least at first, to cope with a trainload of sick and wounded, the casualties were received by the 1st Southern Hospital, Birmingham, and then sent out to the scattered VAD hospitals as soon as their injuries had been assessed. Nevertheless, patients arrived promptly in Kineton - the Herald carries reports of soldiers arriving who "were in the trenches only last week", and overwhelming numbers arrived during July 1916, presumably from the battle of the Somme.

At first, when there were only 20 beds at Clarendon House, almost every arrival and departure is noted in the Kineton column of the Stratford Herald. On 20th November 1914, just after the first contingent of wounded had arrived, the soldiers' regiments are detailed :

Ten came from
the South Wales Borderers   *the Grenadier Guards*
the Ox and Bucks Light Infantry   *the Royal Fusiliers*
the 1st Northamptons   *the Seaforth Highlanders*

Mention is made of "English, Scots, Irish, Welsh and Belgian casualties" and by January 1915 the list of regiments being treated had got so long that after then it was discontinued. The last list[5] given reads :

There are now 23 wounded from
City of London Territorial Force
Queen's Own Royal West Hampshire's
1st and 4th Rifle Brigade
1st and 2nd Royal Dublin Fusiliers
16th Australian Imperial Force
4th Australian Infantry
4th Worcestershire's
Royal Sussex Regiment
4th, 8th and 10th Otago New Zealand Rifles

5th Southland Regiment
Kings Royal Rifles
1st Australian Division
1st Cheshire
2nd East Surrey
1st Hampshire's
4th Northumberland Fusiliers
1st Lincoln

By the end of March 1915 Clarendon House hospital had treated 93 patients, a number exceeded in Warwickshire only by Stratford upon Avon,

Nurses and patients on the steps of Clarendon House Hospital

with its 50 beds.[6]

Expansion plans

In June 1915 the hospital was so busy that the commandants set about finding further accommodation. Mr Fritz Gardner, who left his farm in the hands of a manager and volunteered for service in the early part of the war, kindly agreed to lend his house, then Walton Farm now Walton House, next door to Clarendon House. This allowed another twelve beds to be added to

Walton House, the first extension to the hospital accommodation, taken in 1997. Clarendon House can be seen next door

the hospital, and on 25th June 1915 all the 35 beds then available were full.[7] This number of beds proved adequate for a year, but on 4th August 1916, there was an appeal for volunteers to train as nurses to allow for further expansion of the hospital.

> *Mr and Mrs Fielden have provided rooms at Kineton House, and an additional 15 beds are available, making 50. It is excellent for so small a place as Kineton.*[8]

By March of the following year even greater demand produced yet another response in Kineton.

Kineton House. This building eventually held about 65 beds.

Mrs Fielden is putting 32 beds in the large dining room of Kineton House. She is giving up her sitting room for the surgery, the schoolroom is to be utilised as a sitting room for the soldiers, and two bedrooms will also be used. The additional accommodation will be ready in the course of a week, and the Red Cross hospital will then accommodate 100. The racquet room will be used as a dining room, and it will be in the charge of a sister and a VAD nurse. The household staff will assist in the remainder of the work. A more delightful place could not be found for a hospital.[9]

The hospital accommodation remained at this level until it finally closed on 21st December 1918.

Staffing the hospitals

Finding the staff and providing the training for the number of people needed to run the hospital must have set a challenge to both the administrative team and to Kineton and its neighbouring villages. Three VA detachments were eventually involved. VAD's 8 and 28 (Warwick) were under the commandants Lady Willoughby de Broke and Mrs Fielden, (until ill health forced Lady Willoughby de Broke to retire and Mrs Fielden assumed sole responsibility) with quartermasters the Hon Mabel Verney and Mrs M Pierson-Webber. Lord Willoughby himself was commandant of VAD 3 - an all-male detachment - for a time, and when pressure of work forced him to give up, his place was taken by Guernsey Walsingham Webb, headmaster of a private school in Kineton, organist and churchwarden, who took a leading part in village life. In 1916 each of these detachments consisted of some 20 general staff, making about 60 people involved in all, and by the end of the war the number of staff and helpers that had been active in running the hospital had grown to over 200. Certainly not all these were from Kineton itself, but it is still a remarkable commitment from a village with a population of around 1000.

Courses of lectures given by Dr Price of Banbury Street, Kineton (before he joined the Royal Army Medical Corps in 1917) and Dr Elkington of Fenny Compton, allowed many to obtain their Red Cross qualifications - among them girls too young to receive their certificates though apparently old enough to be allowed on the wards![10]

For the whole of the four years that the hospital was open, the Kineton troop of Boy Scouts provided a scout on daily duty to run errands and act as a messenger to the Commandant.[11]

A Ward, Clarendon House Hospital

Discipline

Little mention is made of the severity of injuries the nurses had to treat, or of how long the soldiers stayed, but much is made of the entertainment and welcome given locally to the in-patients. The freedom given to them undoubtedly led to problems of discipline, and one misdemeanour in 1915 resulted in a court appearance at Kineton petty sessions, at which arrangements at the hospital were scrutinised. One of the soldiers had eluded his escort while out on a walk, and taken the opportunity to get drunk. None of the Kineton landlords would admit to selling him beer - he had apparently persuaded a third party to buy his drinks - and this third party, a groom, William Bishop of Combroke, was summoned that he "being a person on the licensed premises of the Swan Inn, Kineton, did procure certain intoxicating liquor, to wit, one pint of beer, for consumption by a drunken person, Private Frank Williams, 2nd Cheshire Regiment, on September 2nd." On his return to Clarendon House, the soldier "created a disturbance on the wards for nearly three hours after he got back". The magistrates, chaired on this occasion by Mr Ernest Parke of Moorlands Farm, Butlers Marston, decided that Bishop was guilty, but before they passed sentence, Lady Willoughby de Broke, appearing in her position as Commandant of the hospital, asked that the case should be dealt with severely, because

It was a real danger - in some cases almost to life - to soldiers. For one thing it incited them to break away from their escort. Again - and this was a more serious matter - many of these men entered the Hospital with septic wounds, head injuries, brain injuries and so forth, and alcohol might exercise an incalculable amount of bodily harm while they were in this condition. People were making their work at the Hospital much more difficult by encouraging men to break away from their escort, and her Ladyship would be grateful if the bench could make any reference as to this for the welfare of the wounded. Men who got into trouble were, like Williams, sent back to Birmingham in disgrace and put in a solitary ward, and it was one of the most cruel things the public could do to treat them in a manner such as Williams had been treated.[12]

After such a plea by so eminent a person, the bench was not lenient. The groom was fined 40s, and had to pay the expenses of the witnesses attending court, at a time when few workers earned much more than £1 per week[13]. The bench also gave a clear warning that any future cases of this

Lady Willoughby de Broke

kind would meet with a prison sentence.

Despite this case of drunkenness, it seems reasonable to assume that discipline at the hospital was well handled. There is no evidence whatsoever in the parish registers that the close proximity of the community of young soldiers with the young nurses and village girls had any effect on the birthrate, illegitimate or otherwise. Temptation must, however, have been on the minds of those in command at the hospital. In January 1916, some Kineton parishioners were firmly rebuked in the pages of the parish magazine

May we appeal to a small and thoughtless section of our community? A small number of girls in Kineton are making the lot of those responsible for our wounded a very hard one. Their practice is to go out and waylay the men who go for walks. To be friendly and pass the time of day is one thing, to waylay and hinder escorts doing their duty is another. Such conduct shows a lamentable want of self-respect ; those who practice it would be astonished at the strong feeling at the hospital and among the patients and other respectable members of our community, yes, and among the men themselves.[14]

Entertaining the wounded

The majority of soldiers, though, seem to have enjoyed their stay in Kineton's hospital, and, even if romance was discouraged, almost every imaginable entertainment was laid on for them.

There were outings:

The motor rides and many invitations are greatly appreciated by the soldiers. Last week they were invited to Farnborough Hall where they had a splendid time. On Tuesday Mr A Motion of Upton House kindly entertained them, and they landed some fine fish.[15]

They have been to Compton Wynyates and the Round House where Mrs Gaskell of Diana Lodge kindly provided the tea. After a further run to Leamington they returned. They have also been to Avon Dassett - to Bitham House and Avon Carrow.[16]

The round of visiting continues. On Friday, the soldiers attended a conjuring show at the new schools, and tea in the Church rooms. On Saturday there was a concert at Kineton House. On Thursday they went to Stratford-on-Avon to the Christmas tree, and on Saturday and Sunday, Mrs Brand invited them to whist drives and tea. On Monday they gave a concert.[17]

There were Whist Drives in winter and cricket in summer:

On Tuesday afternoon the wounded of Kineton Hospital played the medical officer and staff, the match being witnessed by a large number of spectators. Excitement was aroused when the Honourable Mabel Verney and Dr Elkington went to the wickets, and a very good game followed. The staff scored 63 in two innings, and the patients 65. Miss Carter bowled well. Mrs Gaskell entertained the teams to tea on the ground which they hugely appreciated.[18]

There were concerts, certainly every two weeks, given by Kineton people for the soldiers, and others in which the soldiers entertained their hosts. A series of these concerts took place after the opening of the 'Garland Hall', which was a hut in the grounds of Clarendon House donated by Mr Garland, of Moreton Hall, and fully fitted out with gas lighting and a billiard table. The hut, which was moved to the sports field in Kineton at the end of the war, can still be seen there today in use as a cricket pavilion. All the concerts included singing and sketches, some dancing - "morris dancing by the National School girls"[19] - others conjuring. One concert given by the soldiers was so well received that they repeated it in the Public Hall, and raised £15

A Red Cross certificate, showing the completion of a year's nursing at Clarendon House.

for gramophones for the hospital.[20] The Stratford Herald details many programmes, most of which contain popular songs of the day, many now forgotten. The concert given on Monday, 8th January, 1917 is typical.

> *In the concert given that evening the songs were all well rendered. Messrs. Chandler and Garrett also contributed comic songs which were, as usual, warmly received. One patient's song in particular was loudly applauded. "If I could only make you care" by Private H Hutchinson of the 1st Leicesters, who though he has recently had the misfortune to lose a leg while serving his country, sets a grand example of heroism by his cheerfulness and bravery in his trouble. A sketch specially written for the occasion by Private Porter was well acted and somewhat diverting, the fun arising out of an advertisement for a suitable wife. Justice was done to the respective characters, and the piece seemed to be generally enjoyed.*

Mrs M Baldwin, who nursed at the VAD hospital throughout the war.

Appended is the programme:

Comic song	Driver Wade
Duet	Messrs Chandler and Garrett
Song- *The Wedding of Miss Nightingale*	Sister Hillier
Song- *Trooper Johnnie Ludlow*	Sergeant Dando
Song- *I was Standing at the Corner of the Street*	Mr Garrett
Sketch- *"Seeking a Wife"* - in four acts	
Song- *When You Come Home*	Lance Corporal Thompson
Song- *My Ain Folk*	Sister Hillier
Song- *Off to Philadelphia*	Mr Chandler
Song- *If I Could Only Make You Care*	Private Hutchinson
Song- *I Parted My Hair in the Middle*	Private Sutherland
Song- *Must You Always Have Your Missus With You*	Private A Corrin

A singing of the National Anthem brought the entertainment to a close.[21]

Hospital financing

Whatever the cost of running the hospital, financing all these varied entertainments must have been demanding. For the first six months, the hospital was financed by public subscription with Lady Willoughby de Broke and Mrs Fielden acting as guarantors to cover any deficit.[22] There are constant reports of money raising activities both for the Red Cross movement and for the hospital in Kineton. In the churchwarden's receipts are several signed "Dora Fielden, Commandant" for sums of money from the Church collection plate and from the takings at organ recitals, sums varying from 12s 10d to £8 8s 0d. Entertainments were often generously given in aid of the hospital funds by groups from outside the village, though the Kineton audience still had to dig deep for their admission tickets. One such event had tickets at 5s 0d numbered and reserved, 2s 0d reserved, and 1s 0d or 6d unreserved, at a time when a performance in January 1917 at the Shakespeare Theatre in Stratford-upon-Avon cost 5s 3d for the best front row seats, 3s 9d for the stalls and 7d for the cheapest gallery seats. It was given by the Army Pay Corps, and included a choir of 40 men, humorous items, glees, pianoforte solos and elocutionists, and raised £26

10s 0d.[23]. Another took place in May 1917 when the Kineton Choral Society invited Shipston Choral Society to give a performance of *The Messiah* in St Peter's. It resulted in a profit of £21 10s 0d. for the hospital.

Summer fetes

All these fund raising activities, useful as they undoubtedly were, pale into insignificance when compared to the fund raising fetes held in the summers of 1916 and 1917. The fetes were well advertised and planned. Visitors to the first wartime fete in Kineton were promised the opportunity of meeting Captain Bruce Bairnsfather, a Royal Warwickshire man, best remembered for humorous war cartoons in *The Bystander* involving the character called 'Old Bill'. They were promised countless other attractions, all on the August Bank Holiday that had been officially cancelled because of the war. The people of Warwickshire appear not to have noticed, and poured into Kineton on foot, by bicycle, and by special train.

The pretty grounds of Kineton House (kindly lent by Mr J Fielden) presented an animated and picturesque scene on Monday last, the occasion being a garden fete organised in aid of the Clarendon Red Cross Hospital and War Supply depot. An extensive programme containing a variety of items had been prepared by willing helpers and, favoured by the weather, which could not have been better, the fete proved a big success. Among the numerous attractions offered were concerts, a dramatic sketch, sports, competitions, a Punch-and-Judy show for the entertainment of the children, a palmist etc., while delightful selections were given throughout the afternoon by the Stratford-on-Avon band under the able conductorship of Mr J Cheney. An exhibition of needlework was on show and for sale in the hall, as was a doll's house, the work of Miss Webb's pupils, the models for which were made by Master Fred Griffin, while in the grounds was to be seen a very efficiently furnished first-aid dressing station, erected by Dr Price and Mr Webb. Stalls of all descriptions, and refreshments were dotted here and there in the grounds, ...and the wounded soldiers who were present gave their aid wherever it was needed.

Two well attended concerts were given in the drawing room of Kineton House during the day, presided over by Mr G W Webb at the piano.

The chief item in the programme, that by Captain Bruce Bairnsfather, the popular war cartoonist, was reserved to last...Welcoming him, Mr Webb said the Kineton audience all knew that at the commencement of war, Captain Bairnsfather joined up and went to France : he was blown up, had shell-shock, and came back to England. He returned to France and was at the front at the beginning of the great push which was going on now, but not having fully recovered from the shock he had to come home again on sick-leave. Captain Bairnsfather who appeared by special permission of *The Bystander* then delighted his audience with two of his irresistible lightning sketches, showing the

Bystander copyright.   THE INNOCENT ABROAD
Out since Mons : " Well, what sort of a night 'ave yer 'ad ? "   [again."
Novice (persistent optimist) : " Oh, all right. 'Ad to get out and rest a bit now and

A Bruce Bairnsfather cartoon.

humorous side of life in the trenches. "Ere it is again" and "Watchman, what of the night". Another sketch "A Hopeless Dawn" drawn previous to the concert was also given by the artist. Immediately after these had been passed round for those present to inspect, they were taken outside and sold by auction, where in about ten minutes they had raised the handsome sum of £85. [24]

Afternoon sports were followed by dancing, and, as reported a week later, the sum of £468 14s 8d had been raised.

The 1916 fete was but a preamble to the one held in 1917. In that year the farmers of the area formed a large committee to organise the event, and brought money and new ideas for fund-raising. They invited Miss Mary Anderson, an American actress then living in Broadway, Worcestershire, to open the fete. She was undoubtedly a charismatic figure who had achieved great popularity because of her exceptional beauty, and who, despite her 57 years of age, had just played Juliet in the balcony scene of *Romeo and Juliet* at the London Coliseum. [25] At the concert held at the fete in a huge marquee on the lawn, she recited Lawrence Binyon's poem that is now so well known.

"They shall grow not old
As we that are left grow old;
Age shall not weary them nor years condemn:
On the going down of the sun and in the morning
We will remember them."

In the evening there was a cinema show, and events ended with an auction of gifts donated by the farmers of the neighbourhood. The auction even included a pedigree bull calf presented by Mr Ernest Parke of Moorlands Farm. The result of this massive effort was a sum of £700 for the hospital, and the Stratford Herald of 17th August 1917 carried an editorial to mark the success.

THE KINETON FETE

The most sanguine supporter of this movement could scarcely have expected so splendid a result. But it was well deserved. Everything was admirably conceived, intelligently carried out, and the event took a shape that brought entertainment to a vast number of people. Few expected that from five to six thousand [my italics] people would find their way to the little Warwickshire town now so bereft of Railway accommodation. Had some accurate knowledge of the crowd been formed more bountiful provision would have been made for their personal requirements. The Food Controller, had he been present, would have had an experience that would have been useful to him in his future onerous and not very thankful task. Refreshments were decidedly scarce, and teas had, perforce, to take a rational turn. Many tried the purveyors of the little town to supply their wants, but one and all had gone to the fete, shut up shop, and despised business for the day. Much more money might have been made in the purveying department had there been the slightest premonition of so vast a crowd. But few complaints were forthcoming. Everyone was attracted by a noble cause, and cared little for disappointments of this kind. The result was grand - a sum of £700 for the V A Hospital! The money is wanted. It is an institution that has restored to health and strength many scores of our brave Tommies, and it will continue its fine work while so many generous and patriotic people take a keen interest in its usefulness and efficiency.[26]

With such accolades being heaped upon the village it is perhaps not surprising that the two commandants who had done so much for the hospital both received Honours in 1918. Mrs Dora Fielden was given the OBE in the New Year's Honours List, and Lady Willoughby de Broke the same honour in the Birthday Honours, a little later that year.

The end of the War and a death at the hospital

As the year and the war dragged on, the VAD Hospital continued to treat and entertain patients in the same sort of way. On 11th November, the Armistice was signed, and

the inmates of the hospitals have been especially jubilant this week, and all kinds of amusements have been entered into in honour of the cessation of hostilities.[27]

Then, suddenly, three days later, disaster struck. One of the patients, Corporal Horace Thomas, died. It would appear he was the only patient out of the 2168 wounded who were treated there to die in Kineton. Once again affairs at the hospital were scrutinised in court, and the story of a sad accident came out. Corporal Thomas was a twenty-year old who had been admitted to Clarendon Hospital suffering from shell-shock, and from attacks of giddiness. One evening, when helping to get seats through a trap door into the dining room, for one of the famous concerts, it seems he slipped and

The funeral cortege of Corporal Thomas.

fell, knocking his head. He never regained consciousness. The nurse, Kathleen Boulton (whose parents farmed Battle Farm, now under the Kineton Base Ammunition Depot) had been fetching him some clean collars for the concert, but she was exonerated from blame, and the coroner pronounced himself satisfied that it had been an accident.[28] Nevertheless it must have come a severe blow to the staff of the hospital, and the people of Kineton honoured him as best they could when his coffin was taken to the station for burial at his home in London.

The greatest respect was shown on Tuesday, when the body was taken from the hospital to the station en route for London, blinds being drawn both at the Hospitals and at private houses. The cortège was headed by the Commandant and the sisters and nurses from the Hospitals, while the bier, which contained the remains, was covered with the Union Jack, and upon it rested the deceased's cap. All the soldiers from the Hospitals followed, carrying wreaths. During the latter portion of the journey the coffin was raised shoulder high by six of the deceased's comrades, and, as it reached the station, the rest of the soldiers formed a guard of honour, standing at the salute. Floral tributes were sent by the Commandant (Mrs Fielden), Section staff and men, Q.M. The Hon Mabel

Verney, Clarendon staff and men, Kineton House staff and men, etc.[29]

The hospital closed down for Christmas 1918 on 20th December, and never reopened.

Honours for the hospital team

All 200 of the hospital staff, the patients, and those who had in any way helped with the work of caring for the wounded, including sisters, laundry workers, and orderlies, were entertained in the Public Hall to refreshments, cigars and cigarettes, by Mrs Fielden and her team at the beginning of 1919.

In September 1919 many of the hospital staff received certificates signed by Queen Alexandra in recognition of their work.[30]

Mrs Fielden	Mrs M Wade	Mrs Lakin
Miss M Freeman	Miss Potter	Miss L Willock
The Hon M Verney	Mrs M Baldwin	Mr Orme Tiley
Dr Oldmeadow	Mrs Woodfield	Dr Elkington
Mrs M Holbech	Miss Moore	Miss M Carter
Miss E Smith	Mrs Waldron	Miss G Smith
Lady Willoughby de Broke	Miss M Goulder	Mr G W Webb
Miss M W Holbech		

The certificates were presented at a function organised to mark the closure of the VAD Hospitals in Kineton. Those present were addressed by Lady Willoughby de Broke, who as well as thanking everyone for their sterling effort during the war, exhorted them all to continue with their valuable Red Cross work. The editorial in the Stratford Herald echoes her praises.

'Well done, Kineton Division!' These words with which Lady Willoughby de Broke concluded her admirable address yesterday form a fitting commentary on the War Record of this pretty Warwickshire town. Situated in the centre of England, it has given from its heart men to fight by land, sea, and air : money to provide the sinews of war, and women who have thrown themselves whole-heartedly into the task of nursing our wounded heroes back to health [31]

Mrs Fielden then thanked all who had worked at the hospital during the war, mentioning particularly the doctors and the Quartermasters who had taken charge of 110 or so people so well. She concluded by reading highly appreciative letters of thanks from the Administrator of the 1st Southern General Hospital and from the headquarters of the Southern Command.

The third speaker was Mabel Verney. She started by saying how sorry she was when Lady Willoughby was obliged to retire owing to ill-health. She continued

Mrs Fielden (who continued as Commandant alone) had the courtesy and graciousness to consult Lady Willoughby on every point. They worked in perfect accord the whole of the time, but naturally the lion's share of the work fell to Mrs Fielden and she did not think any VAD hospital could have been worked more successfully than the one at Kineton. They all loved respected and looked up to her; and they had also to thank Mr Fielden, who not only gave his house and time, but something he liked better than anything, his wife. For four years he was shoved in the corner and put on one side, and had to find consolation by working in the kennels from morning to night... She now had the greatest pleasure in asking Mrs Fielden's acceptance of a convertible pendant-brooch (rubies and diamonds), together with a cheque, and a scroll (written by Mr Guernsey Webb) containing the names of 100 subscribers. Mrs Fielden received an ovation.[52]

One of the certificates presented to Kineton VAD nurses at the end of the war, bearing the signature of the Queen.

Hospital honours at the Parish Church

A year after the end of the war, the flags which had hung so proudly over the hospital were placed in the church as a permanent memorial.

The members of the Red Cross formed up outside the late Clarendon Hospital for church parade, headed by their Commandants, the Lady Willoughby de Broke OBE of the 8th division, and Mrs Fielden OBE of the 28th division, bearing the flags. Besides the members of the Red Cross, the ex-servicemen, the Comrades of the Great War, were especially invited to attend, and turned out in large numbers, also the boy scouts. Mr Webb presided at the organ, Colonel B Hanbury read the lessons, and the Vicar gave an excellent address.

At the end of the service

the Vicar proceeded to the altar, followed by the commandants carrying the flags. These were handed to the Vicar, who placed them on the altar and blessed them. They are to be fixed on the capitals of pillars each side of the chancel arch.[33]

Whether they were placed in that position is not recorded, but certainly they both hung for many years in the church on both sides of the brass war-memorial plaque, where indeed one hangs to this day. Sadly, few remember why.

1 *Parish Magazine*, February 1910
2 ibid., November 1910
3 Report of the British Red Cross Society, 31 March 1916, pp. 12-25
4 ibid., p.32
5 *Stratford upon Avon Herald*, 28 May 1915
6 *Warwickshire Advertiser*, 8 May 1915
7 *Stratford upon Avon Herald*, 25 June 1915
8 ibid., 4 August 1916
9 ibid., 16 March 1917
10 ibid., 31 December 1915, 26 May 1916, 4 August 1916 etc.
11 *Parish Magazine,* February 1919
12 *Warwickshire Advertiser*, 1 October 1915
13 **Stevenson, John**. *British Society* 1914-45 (Allen Lane : 1984) p.79
14 *Parish Magazine*, January 1916
15 *Stratford upon Avon Herald*, 28 May 1915
16 ibid., 11 June 1915
17 ibid., 12 January 1917

18 ibid., 17 August 1917
19 ibid., 17 December 1915
20 ibid., 25 October 1918
21 ibid., 12 January 1917
22 *Parish Magazine*, May 1915
23 ibid., January 1917
24 *Stratford upon Avon Herald*, 11 August 1916
25 *Encyclopaedia Britannica*; also *Who's Who in the Theatre*, 1912-1976
     (Pitman : 1978) p.48
26 *Stratford upon Avon Herald*, 17 August 1917
27 ibid., 15 November 1918
28 ibid., 22 November 1918
29 ibid., 22 November 1918
30 ibid., 21 February 1919 and 28 February 1919; also 5 September 1919
31 ibid., 21 February 1919
32 ibid., 28 February 1919
33 ibid., 14 November 1919

Chapter Four
Celebrating Peace

The end of the War

Rejoicing at the prospect of peace began the day the armistice was signed.

The official news of this important event reached Kineton shortly before mid-day, and led to great rejoicing. Flags were hoisted in various parts of the town, merry peals were rung on the bells, and the hospitals received very generous decoration. Every one was in the highest spirits and general were the congratulations on the great victory of the Allies. A thanksgiving service was held at St Peter's church shortly after noon, and a large congregation was present, including members of other denominations. The service opened with the playing of the National Anthem, and suitable hymns followed. The Rev C Jickling, vicar-in-charge, officiated, and delivered a very practical address from the chancel steps, basing his discourse on the Song of Solomon, 7th verse.* He referred to the sad losses that had been locally sustained, and remarked that there would be many vacant chairs in the homes of the people. Let them pray that their souls would rest in Paradise. The Te Deum was heartily sung as an act of thanksgiving.[1]

By February 1919 it was reported that a great many of the soldiers had returned to their homes, and "looked very well satisfied with the change of events."[2] Despite the signing of the Armistice, the Peace Treaties were not signed until June 1919, and not ratified until 31st August, 1921. The war with Turkey was not officially declared at an end until 1924, all of which explains the variation in dates for hostilities on War Memorials up and down the country.[3] In Kineton, even church plaques and the War Memorial accredit different dates.

* No Chapter number is given, and it is difficult to find a suitable verse 7 in the Song of Solomon to be used as a text. The well known Chapter 2, v 11 - 12 seems more likely.

A "Peace" card.

Official peace celebrations

A national thanksgiving service took place in St Peter's Church on Sunday, 6th July, 1919, by which time the plans for a peace celebration for the whole village were well advanced. In the event these plans were somewhat curtailed by the weather, but a flavour of the patriotism felt in the country at that time, and of the cohesion that had characterised so much of the war effort in Kineton, is given by the report in the Stratford Herald.

The most complete preparations were made for duly celebrating peace on Saturday, but the rain greatly marred the proceedings. The Public-hall was kindly lent by Mrs Hiatt, and this was very gaily decorated and made quite a festive scene in itself. Here a bountiful dinner was provided by the committee, Mr Trenfield serving up a very generous repast. That full justice was done to the viands goes without saying. The company mainly comprised all the soldiers, sailors and airmen who had been demobilised [this would have been about 200 men] and they made up a merry party. The toast list was a very patriotic one. In proposing the King, Queen and Royal Family, the Chairman commented on the fine example the King and Queen had set their subjects during the war, and the Prince of Wales had won popularity by his activities among the people and also as an officer...In submitting the Army, Navy and Air Forces, the Chairman welcomed those present as representing the lads of Kineton, and thanked them for all they had done for them during the war. He said they must not only thank the men for winning the war, but also God, for on several occasions it was a higher power than man that ruled the victories - 'To those who had made the great sacrifice'. All stood silent a minute to honour those who were not there.... Mr Chandler welcomed the men home, and hoped the single ones would soon find work, and in a few years, plenty of houses, where they might have happy homes similar to the married ones of today.

A move was made to the recreation ground, where numerous sports were entered into, young and old alike taking part. Each of the youngsters received a medal to remind them of the event. Money prizes were also given. Tea followed and this proved a rather important function, as all were invited to participate in this popular refreshment.

At this point rain interrupted the events, and on Monday:

A large concourse of people assembled to witness them [the sports and dancing]. Glad the people were to welcome the Rev W H B Yerburgh, and among those present were Mr and Mrs Holbech, the Hon Mrs B Hanbury (a sister of Lord Willoughby) Mrs

A membership certificate of the Comrades of the Great War, Kineton branch. Note the signature of W H B Yerburgh.

Gaskell, Mr F G Sumner, Dr Oldmeadow etc. These did all in their power to make the enjoyment complete. The sports passed off most successfully, the events being watched with much interest. Dancing afforded a pleasant item, being spiritedly entered into, and a display of fireworks brought to a close a very interesting celebration.[4]

The fireworks were donated by a farmer, refreshments were given by Messrs Hunt, Edmonds and Co., owners of the Swan and the Rose and Crown, and produced by their landlords, and the rest of the funds were raised by a house to house collection. This produced £88 14s 9d, and after expenses of £77 10s 2d had been deducted, the remaining £11 4s 7d was given to Kineton lads still serving in the forces.[5]

But a day of celebration was not enough. In Kineton - just as all over the country - people felt the need for a permanent reminder of all that they had been through, a need which was to be met by the planning and building of the War Memorial.

1   *Stratford upon Avon Herald*, 15 November 1918
2   ibid., 7 February 1919
3   **McIntyre, Colin.** *Monuments of War*, (Hale : 1990), p.29
4   *Stratford upon Avon Herald*, 25 July 1919
5   ibid., 1 August 1919

Chapter Five
The Building of the War Memorial

Choosing a memorial

The first mention of plans to build a memorial to the fallen of the First World War is made in March 1919, some four months after the end of hostilities, at a time when not all serving soldiers had yet returned home.

A public meeting was held to assess support, chaired by Lord Willoughby de Broke, who was both the Lord of the Manor, an active member of the House of Lords, and a former commander of the Warwickshire Yeomanry. Lord Willoughby's plan was to collect ideas, and, subject to the approval of those present, to form a committee to deal with the matter.

> *"They had three points to consider", he said. " 'If at all,' 'what form,' and 'choosing the committee.'"*[1]

It would appear from the lengthy report of this meeting that there was no lack of ideas. Mr Hutton, Lord Willoughby's agent from Pittern Hill, proposed

> *a cross at the top of Bridge street and a tablet in the church, which would serve to remind them in years to come what others had done before them.*

Mr Fisher, a staunch Methodist, (five of whose sons had served in the War, two of them losing their lives), elaborated on this idea, suggesting

> *a good block of Edgehill stone, with table top and the figure of a soldier with scroll in hand, bearing the names of the fallen, should be erected on the site opposite Mr Lewis's shop. It would be a great attraction, and if, at the end of each portion, a little fir tree was planted, its picturesqueness would be much enhanced. The site Mr Hutton had mentioned would, he was afraid, prove very inconvenient, as there was not much space. Near the Wesleyan chapel was another site, which would be suitable, and also add to the beauty of the town.*

The site 'opposite Mr Lewis's shop' is indeed where the memorial stands to this day.

The site of the War Memorial, before it was built. In the background can be seen the chemist's shop run by the Bancrofts. The three Bancroft sons went to fight in the war, and all returned safely.

Mr Chandler pointed out that any obstruction in the road at the top of Bridge street would be hazardous to the increasing amount of motor car traffic, and threw in his own idea for "a big hall", admitting none the less that "they would have as much as they could do to build houses and that money would be scarce for some time." Chandler was a relatively common name in Kineton at this period, and it is not clear from the records which of them was speaking - the National schoolmaster, the Southam Street butcher or the Banbury Street tailor - but he was certainly a man of admirable foresight to foresee the traffic problems of the late twentieth century.

Mr Gilks said that he would like to see a cottage hospital, which could be called the War Memorial Hospital, and easily supported by the proceeds of an annual fete. (Kineton certainly had a superb reputation for successfully organising fetes at that time, attracting up to 6000 people to them and able to raise £700, as in 1918)

An attempt by Lord Willoughby to adjudicate between the ideas was quickly squashed. Any team spirit engendered during the war quickly evaporated. Lord Willoughby was accused of being out of touch with the common, poorer people, who had more need of reading and recreation rooms than memorials. Less ambitious ideas soon followed. Perhaps not surprisingly, Mr Geden, the saddler and harness maker, thought that a horse trough would be a fitting monument to the horses who had done their share in wartime, and the Hon Mrs Hanbury, Lord Willoughby's sister, wanted "a little trough for dogs".

Order was restored, tempers cooled, and the committee was elected "with the power to add to its number".
It consisted of :-
Lord Willoughby de Broke
the Hon Mabel Verney
Mr Fisher (draper)
Mr Hooten (farmer)
Mr Brisker (builder)

A Cottage hospital?

The principal ideas, then, were for a cottage hospital or for a memorial. By May the committee had chosen a memorial, but the idea of a cottage hospital did not go away. The Parish Council minutes dated 26th September, 1919, appoint Mr Sumner, J.P., as their representative on the Cottage Hospital committee "if such be formed". The Stratford Herald reports progress on the plans for a cottage hospital throughout October and November 1919. The proposed scheme envisaged a building for the use of villagers living in the Kineton petty sessional division, to be built in Southam road, in Bath stone, and staffed with the help of the VAD, many of whom were resident in Kineton and thought to be willing "to render assistance".[2]
The following week, the Stratford Herald was even more positive:

The scheme for a cottage hospital in Kineton is nearly complete. In addition to public wards it is to have a private ward. The promoters are wisely having the plans prepared in such a way that the hospital could be added to at any time, and the wards arranged to reduce labour to a minimum. Cottage hospitals are a great success nowadays wherever they are established and the ladies and gentlemen of Kineton have had such experience during the war in hospital work, that it is felt such an institution could not be in better hands. We understand there will be no central heating apparatus, it being considered that patients will be more cheerful in wards with ordinary fires. The hospital will be built on the Southam Road which has the great advantage of being near a doctor's residence.[3]

Exactly one week later the Herald announced

After all the new cottage hospital will not be built in Kineton.

It is not known whether this hospital was ever built elsewhere, nor what provoked such a sudden about-turn. An architect, Mr Knight of Stratford-upon-Avon, is named in one of the reports[4] but the plans do not appear to have survived. John H Knight, whose premises were in Rother Street, continued to practice in Stratford for many years, and was made Mayor of the borough in 1940.

Brigstock Market Cross and Kineton War Memorial compared.

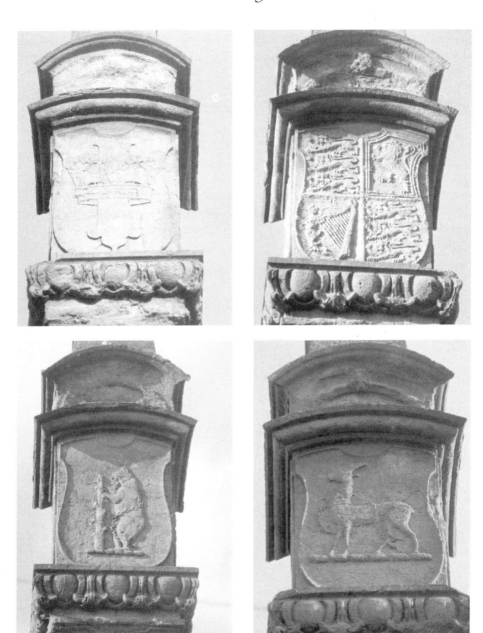

The War Memorial Carvings: The Naval Crown; The Royal Coat of Arms; The Bear and Ragged Staff of the Warwickshire Yeomanry; The Antelope for the Royal Warwickshire Regiment.

The final plan

Nevertheless, despite all this, there seems to have been no doubt in the minds of the committee that a decision to build a monument had been reached, and plans were more or less finalised at a second public meeting on Monday 26th May, 1919. Lord Willoughby de Broke, once again in the Chair, submitted the following ideas for the meeting to consider.

No. 1 plan.... presented the figure of a soldier in uniform on a pedestal, with names carved thereon. To carry this out in Portland stone the cost would be £512, which would include everything but the understructure. It would be liable to suffer from exposure. A hand in time might get broken off or the features disfigured. He for one would not recommend it in stone. The same in bronze would cost £761 9s 0d, a large sum, and it was risky, in his humble opinion, to introduce this new element into Kineton. The alternative to this, which he ventured to think was dignified, artistic, and suitable to Kineton - and one of the committee, Mr Hutton, had been fortunate to see it at Brigstock - was a market cross. This, if carried out in Hornton stone, to include brass memorial tablets in church and chapel, would cost £300, but this sum did not include railings. The names of the fallen would be inscribed on the memorial as well as in church and chapel. Perhaps they would like something more simple altogether.⁵

As in every village meeting, now and in 1919, a certain amount of tut-tutting over the cost and minor details took place, but by show of hands it was decided unanimously to erect a cross similar to that at Brigstock, Northamptonshire, with three feet plain at the foot for names, a cross at the summit instead of a weather vane, and carvings on each of its four sides. These carvings were to be a Naval Crown for the senior service, a Royal Coat of Arms for the soldiers and, on the remaining two sides, the arms of the local regiments, a Bear and Ragged Staff for the Warwickshire Yeomen, and an antelope for the Royal Warwickshire Regiment. The eventual success of this design can be seen in the centre of Kineton today, but who was the architect, and why the design should be based on an obscure market cross in Brigstock, remain a mystery. The builders, J F Booth and Son, of Edgehill, were appointed by 14th April, 1920. The firm survives today as Hornton Stone Quarries, and they have in their possession several albums of photographs of War Memorials they constructed in the 1920s. They include

IN THANKFUL & PROUD
MEMORY
OF THE
MEN OF KINETON
WHO FOUGHT AND DIED
FOR KING & COUNTRY
IN THE GREAT WAR
1914 – 1918
THESE NOBLY PLAYED THEIR PART
THESE HEARD THE CALL
FOR GOD & KING & HOME
THEY GAVE THEIR ALL

PETTY OFFICER	G.H. BALDWIN R.N.
CAPTAIN	R.W. FISHER
" "	R.F. SMITH M.C.
LIEUT.	P.W. FISHER D.C.M.
" "	D.G. SMITH M.C.
SERGT.	C.A. HUDSON
" "	G.F. PLUMMER
" "	J. WHEILDON
CORPL.	J. COLEMAN
" "	C.M.M. ELLICK
L/CPL	J.E.W. COLLETT
" "	K. GREEN
" "	J.W. HORSLEY

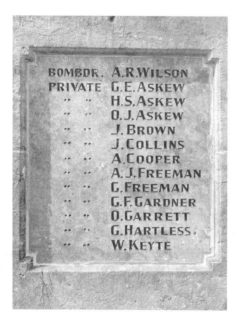

BOMBDR.	A.R. WILSON
PRIVATE	G.E. ASKEW
" "	H.S. ASKEW
" "	O.J. ASKEW
" "	J. BROWN
" "	J. COLLINS
" "	A. COOPER
" "	A.J. FREEMAN
" "	G. FREEMAN
" "	G.F. GARDNER
" "	O. GARRETT
" "	G. HARTLESS
" "	W. KEYTE

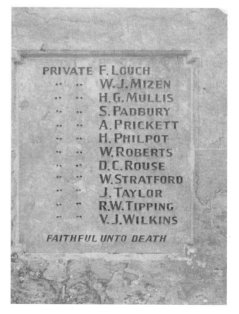

PRIVATE	F. LOUCH
" "	W.J. MIZEN
" "	H.G. MULLIS
" "	S. PADBURY
" "	A. PRICKETT
" "	H. PHILPOT
" "	W. ROBERTS
" "	D.C. ROUSE
" "	W. STRATFORD
" "	J. TAYLOR
" "	R.W. TIPPING
" "	V.J. WILKINS

FAITHFUL UNTO DEATH

The inscriptions

not only memorials, as one would expect, in many of the surrounding Warwickshire villages, like Butlers Marston, Northend, Shuckborough, and the much moved memorial in Stratford-upon Avon, but also such prestigious monuments as the one at Christchurch, Oxford, that in Chippenham (one of the most beautiful in the West Country according to a leading daily paper), and the memorial erected at the Royal Staff College to commemorate the graduates who fell in the war, which contains the names of some of Britain's most famous soldiers.[6] That, together with the fact that Hornton stone was specified by such illustrious architects of the day as Sir Edwin Lutyens and George Gilbert Scott, and was used for the much admired sundial presented to Princess Mary on the occasion of her wedding in 1922, suggests that the stone was fashionable and much in demand. Such demand may even explain why the Rugby Advertiser reported in May 1921 that

> *after many delays, the carving of the War Memorial will be completed next week. The erection will be proceeded with forthwith, and it is expected that the opening ceremony will take place on the last Sunday in June.*[7]

By this time many villages had already unveiled memorials and yet it is hard to accuse Kineton, who had started planning so soon, of being tardy. Of the twenty-one villages in the Kineton deanery, fourteen dedicated their war memorials before Kineton, even though many of them had not started planning and raising money until well into the beginning of 1920. For example, Hornton stone monuments were unveiled in Fenny Compton in February, in Combroke in March, and in Lighthorne in August, all in 1920. Lighthorne does report that

> *The carrying out of the Lighthorne memorial has taken much more time than expected. Mr Pullin of Leamington Spa, who has the work in hand, has had great difficulty in obtaining the stone from Hornton Quarry.*[8]

Dedication of the plaques

The brass plaques planned as part of the memorial to men of Kineton were the first to be ready. It was decided to unveil the one in St Peter's parish church at a confirmation service to be conducted by the Bishop of Coventry. Consequently, reports the Parish Magazine,

Later in the evening [2nd December, 1920] the Bishop dedicated the Memorial Brass placed in our church to the memory of the men from the parish who fell during the Great War. What a touching and beautiful service it was! Not only pathetic and solemn, but also with the ring of faith and hope which should be present. Lord Willoughby de Broke performed the ceremony of unveiling, which was followed by the Dedication and special prayers. The Rural Dean read the lesson. The musical portions of the service were rendered beautifully. It was such a pleasure to find the Rev W H B Yerburgh with us. [9]

By this time, the Rev W H B Yerburgh was the incumbent of the church at Bredon, Worcestershire, and he must have come specially to attend the dedication.

Dedication of the wayside memorial

Seven months later, the imposing new monument at the centre of the village was ready for the dedication ceremony on Sunday, 10th July, 1921.

The service opened in the Parish church, before moving to the memorial, only about two hundred yards away. Two former vicars of Kineton had returned for the ceremony and led the procession. One, the Rev A H Watson, had been Vicar of Kineton from 1890-94 and was then Rector of Lighthorne, and the other was the Rev W H B Yerburgh. Drawn up round the monument, together with many parishioners, were relatives of the fallen, ex-servicemen, churchwardens, sidesmen, girl guides and the members of the committee, now with Joshua Fielden, whose home, Kineton House, had been used throughout the War as a VAD hospital, as their chairman. The service was conducted jointly by the vicar, the Rev Hugh Holbech, and the Wesleyan minister, the Rev T E Brigden, and the singing, which was described as "a feature of the ceremony", was led by the church choir and a ladies choir, under the direction of Mr Guernsey Walsingham Webb.

The formal unveiling was done by General Gage (of Farnborough) whose address concluded with the words

In memory of those gallant British soldiers of Kineton in whom we placed our trust, and who could not fail us, I have the honour to unveil the memorial of your respect and gratitude for duty well and nobly done. [10]

Buglers from Budbrooke Barracks sounded the *Last Post*, and after the

KINETON, WARWICKSHIRE.

THESE FELL IN THE GREAT WAR, 1914—1919.

Petty Officer G. H. BALDWIN, R.N.
Captain R. W. FISHER.
,, R. F. SMITH, M.C.
Lieut. P. W. FISHER, D.C.M.
,, D. G. SMITH, M.C.
Sergt. C. A. HUDSON.
,, G. F. PLUMMER.
,, J. WHEILDON.
Corpl. J. G. COLEMAN.
,, C. M. M. ELLICK.
Lc.-Corpl. J. E. W. COLLETT.
,, K. GREEN.
,, J. HORSLEY.
Bombr. A. R. WILSON.
Private G. E. ASKEW.
,, H. S. ASKEW.
,, O. J. ASKEW.
,, J. BROWN.

Private J. COLLINS.
,, A. COOPER.
,, A. J. FREEMAN.
,, G. FREEMAN.
,, G. F. GARDNER.
,, O. GARRETT.
,, G. HARTLESS.
,. W. KEYTE.
.. F. LOUCH.
., W. J. MIZEN.
,, H. G. MULLIS.
,, S. PADBURY.
,, A. PRICKETT.
,, H. PHILPOT.
,, W. ROBERTS.
,, D. C. ROUSE.
,, W. STRATFORD.
,, J. TAYLOR.
,, R. W. TIPPING.

Private V. J. WILKINS.

The Unveiling & Dedication

OF

THE WAYSIDE MEMORIAL CROSS,

BY

The Right Rev. The LORD BISHOP OF COVENTRY

And GENERAL GAGE,

On SUNDAY, JULY 10th, 1921.

" Greater love hath no man than this, that a man lay down his life for his friends."

These nobly played their part, these heard the call,
For God and King and Home they gave their all.

The programme for the Dedication Ceremony

The Unveiling, Sunday July 10, 1921

Antiphon *Give to thy Servants rest with Thy Saints*, the Bishop of Coventry led a simple dedication service. A large number of wreaths were placed on the memorial, including those from relatives, the War Memorial committee and the Oddfellows.

Final administration

The final meeting of the War Memorial Committee took place on Monday, 18th September 1922. At it the audited accounts were presented to the committee, Mr J Fielden (Chairman), Mr J Griffin (Hon Sec), Mr F G Sumner, Mr R Brisker, Mr J Fisher, and the Hon Mabel Verney, and they decided that the remaining balance should be used for the future improvement of the War Memorial. [11]

Certainly a low wall was put round the Memorial at a later date, and in March 1947 it was announced that "a local fund" would be used to have the names of those who fell in World War Two inscribed on the War Memorial.[12]

1   *Stratford upon Avon Herald*, 21 March 1919
2   ibid., 3 October 1919
3   ibid., 17 October 1919

4   ibid., 7 November 1919
5   ibid., 30 May 1919
6   *The Stone Trades Journal*, January 1923
7   *Rugby Advertiser*, 27 May 1921
8   *Parish Magazine*, June 1920
9   ibid., January 1921
10 *Stratford upon Avon Herald*, 15 July 1921
11 ibid., 22 September 1922
12 ibid., 28 March 1947

Chapter Six
After the War

Many soldiers who returned home after the war had been changed and scarred for ever, some physically, others mentally. It is only in very recent years that an effort has been made to recognise and treat by counselling the mental trauma caused by horrific experiences. Such treatment was certainly not available to the vast majority of soldiers, although efforts to understand what is loosely called "shell-shock" were made early in the war at specialist hospitals like Craiglockhart, and the subject has been dealt with graphically by Pat Barker in the *Regeneration* trilogy.

There is nobody who fought in the Great War still living in Kineton now, but the relatives of the soldiers, their children, their nephews and nieces, are, without exception, adamant that their fathers and uncles rarely spoke of their experiences. It would be comforting to think that the soldiers returned to an easy life in a land of plenty, and it is hard to accept that the war had caused changes at home which meant that too often work was scarce, money was very tight even for those in employment, and the prospects for a man crippled in the service of his country were grim. Their children, for the most part, remember hard times.

Prospects, though, might have been slightly better in Kineton than in some other places, for the Warwickshire Hunt was about to enjoy a golden age of prosperity and to become, in the years immediately after the War, one of the most fashionable packs in the country. The wealthy continued to come and live in Kineton for the hunting season, and brought trade to the village shops and craftsmen, and plenty of work for those in service. The people who had led the village so successfully through the war years were still at the head of village affairs, but it was a time of surprisingly rapid change in almost every way.

Within five years, Lord Willoughby de Broke had died and been succeeded by his son ; Guernsey Walsingham Webb and Joseph Chandler had left their respective schools, and indeed the village, Mr Webb for ordination into the Anglican church at the age of 57, and Mr Chandler for retirement ; and the wartime vicar of St Peter's had gone to Bredon.

On the other hand, though Joshua Fielden soon gave up the Mastership of the Warwickshire Hunt, he was to remain in Kineton for many more years.

So too did his wife, whose contribution to the village and county organisations had only just begun. Lord Willoughby's relatives, the Honourable Mabel Verney, and her niece the Honourable Patience Hanbury, also remained in the village after the war, and were active in village life.

Brief biographies of these and some other Kineton personalities who had served the village during the War are in Part Two.

*****

Few Kineton residents would claim that Kineton has ever been anything but an ordinary English village, and this history does not seek to change that judgement. The words of the scroll given to the family of every soldier who died for his country ask:

"Let those who come after see to it that his name be not forgotten"

The rest of this book, therefore, is devoted to naming and recording those who gave so generously in the service of their country, whether in the Forces or at home in Kineton. A few, through their letters home, have left us vivid insights into their experiences, and have ensured their memorial ; I have tried to see that none are now forgotten.

PART TWO - Kineton People

Chapter Seven
The Soldiers and Sailors of the Village

Much has been written about the horrors of the Great War. The autobiographies of soldiers of all ranks, the eloquence of war poets like Siegfried Sassoon and Wilfred Owen, and, later, histories, novels, plays, films and television documentaries have all sought ways to show the reality of life in the trenches. The evidence that survives in Kineton is on a less heroic scale, but still it paints the picture of a village caught up in events undreamed of when war broke out. Even in so undramatic an English village, the horror of what was happening changed life for the ordinary person for ever.

The Vicar, a Naval chaplain

The vicar, the Rev William Higgin Beauchamp Yerburgh, despite being in a profession that was exempt from service in the Forces, announced to his parishioners in church on 28th January 1916 that the Bishop had granted him a year's leave of absence to enable him to accept a post of Naval Chaplain on a battleship. Two weeks later he went to be chaplain on the *Drake*. At first, aged 35, he found the life stimulating and enjoyable.

My dear friends

....With regard to my work I may say very little since the censorship is so strict. When this reaches you I shall have been many thousands of miles, and seen a great deal of life in one of our large ships. The Padre, as I am called, censors letters, 'codes and decodes' at all hours, is with the doctor's party in action, takes the services and daily prayers, and superintends the school, organises the concert party and visits the sick ward. I have a good organist, I think, but not a Mr Webb, and a good schoolmaster, but not a Mr Chandler. People at home should see a little of naval life and they would appreciate some of the hardships. The following is a sample : on a certain ship where no fresh food had been for some time, a leg of mutton was sent for the officers, when a wave caught the cook, and it was swept away. Then the voice of a man at a gun was

W H B Yerburgh, in his naval uniform

heard saying 'Here, take your dinner from under my foot' and they did so and what is more ate it. My first communion service was in a casemate by a big gun, the altar and cloths made for me looked very nice....

Your affectionate vicar
W.H.B Yerburgh [1]

Later letters, in July and August 1916, read:

The weather is much better now; and the men will have an easier time. We are organising boxing, football and concert parties when we are ashore. Our work is varied and we are frequently running the gauntlet of subs. but so far have been unmolested. There is a good deal of fun and good fellowship in the wardroom. We are not, I fear, 'grand and reverent signors', the padre must be prepared to 'scrap' and be 'skiffed', to attempt somersaults and other things that might appear undignified at vestry meeting, but which are not out of place here. [2]

On the only occasion he helped to coal ship, and the last, you would not have recognised the Vicar of Kineton, but would have asked the blackened figure to deposit your coals in the cellar, and given him twopence for doing it. [3]

There is then a long silence from the Vicar, though parishioners received regular reports of his career. He was torpedoed off the Giants Causeway in October 1917, and then commissioned to *HMS Campania*. That, too, was sunk (in the Firth of Forth in November 1918), and after visiting the parish, he sounded a little reluctant to be sent back into service on *HMS Queen*, the flagship in the Mediterranean, where he stayed until June 1919. He had written from the *Campania* just before she was sunk

Now every time one goes ashore there is a sea trip of some two miles in a motor boat built for Thames backwaters, to which one clings for dear life when wind and tide create a nasty sea. True, there are compensations! We do get two boxes of matches a week! 8oz of sugar! and we do have lots of coal, which means a hot bath and steam heating, but when I tell you I actually enjoyed my time of waiting in the dental sitting room because there were pictures on the wall, real windows and a genuine carpet, you will understand we will not be sorry when another spell of leave comes our way. [4]

The Rev W H B Yerburgh may have found his naval experiences arduous, but it is reasonable to think that, with the benefit of his up-bringing and education, he had travelled and maybe even been abroad before he joined up. Some of the young volunteers would have seen a lot less of life, and may never have left the village before. Their accounts of experiences, printed in the Parish Magazine, are eloquent, and worthy of Yerburgh's pride and confidence in the village schoolmaster, Mr Chandler.

The Wisdom family

The young Harry Wisdom, who had been the only one to volunteer at the recruiting meeting in December 1914, wrote home the sort of letter one might hope to receive from a son.

Thank you for the nice things you sent me. The pork pie, cake, chocs, tarts, etc were a real treat. Dear Mother and Pap I know you worry, but don't, as I know it is God's will I shall come out quite safe and we cannot do anything else but put our life in his hands and trust in him. He has always been a great help to me and always will be.[5]

Harry Wisdom's faith was rewarded. Though he was wounded in France twice while serving with the Rifle Brigade, and had spells in hospital in Boulogne and, more seriously, in Leicester, he arrived home safely at the end of the war, with the rank of Corporal and complete with the Distinguished Conduct Medal. His elder brother Martin also came home safely, having been in the Royal Engineers. Both Martin and Harry followed their father into the family business as carpenters, a business which has been responsible for much of the modern woodwork and pews in St Peter's church. The third of the Wisdom brothers, William, worked a $46\frac{1}{2}$ acre farm on the Lighthorne Road, and because of this, and because his two brothers were in the army, he was given exemption from military service by the tribunal in Stratford.

A last letter from the Front

Lance Corporal Ernest Collett of the 3rd Worcester's sent a poem written at the Front in his letter home only days before he was killed in action. It was printed in the Parish Magazine in January 1916. There is no indication there whether it was a completely original poem, or adapted from one circulating amongst the troops. It appears to be based on a popular song, an idea supported by four very similar lines used in the musical *Oh What A Lovely*

War (Theatre Workshop, first performance March 1963) It is interesting to see that in the first stanza the pronunciation of Ypres as Wipers seems much the most likely.

Sing Me To Sleep

Sing me to sleep where bullets fall,
Let me forget the war and all;
Damp is my dug-out, cold are my feet;
Nothing but bully and biscuit to eat;
Sing me to sleep where bombs explode
And shrapnel shells are à la mode,
Over the sandbags helmets you'll find,
Corpses in front of you, corpses behind.
    Far, far from Ypres I long to be,
    Where German snipers can't pot at me,
    Think of me crouching where worms do creep,
    Waiting for someone to put me to sleep.

Sing me to sleep in some old shed,
A dozen rat-holes round my head;
Stretched out on my waterproof
Dodging the rain drops from the roof;
Sing me to sleep where camp-fires glow,
Full of French bread and café à l'eau
Dreaming of home and nights in the west
Somebody's overseas boots on my chest.
    Far, far from Plug Street I long to be,
    Lights of old Kineton I'd rather see;
    Think of me crouching where worms do creep
    Waiting for Sergeant to sing me to sleep.[6]

Lance Corporal J E W Collett died on December 11th 1915, aged 21. He is buried at Prowse Point Cemetery, just outside Ypres, not far from Ploegsteert, (Plug Street).

The grave of J E W Collett at Prowse Point Cemetery. The great "Cross of Sacrifice" designed by Sir Reginald Blomfield RA is clearly visible. This cross has been erected at all official British and Commonwealth cemeteries abroad, and is the model used for many War Memorials up and down the country.

Air Warfare

J A Cowley wrote a vivid description of the horrors of the front line in a letter to his parents which was quoted in the Parish Magazine of December 1915. It can have done nothing for their peace of mind - but he arrived home safely.

My dear Father and Mother

....I am getting quite used to dodging Jack Johnsons and Black Maria's, and Whistling Rufus's as we call them, we make fun of them now, if they don't put one close to us, and call them bad shots, we know if one does drop on us our time is up, but we never think about that, so long as we can send them a few to be going on with.

....I saw a good bit of sport yesterday afternoon with one of our aeroplanes and one of

the Germans; the German plane was coming over our guns, we fired a few rounds at him and turned him off, then one of our aeroplanes spotted him and they had a fight in the air and ours came off best, they were about 4000 yards up and our fellow put a maxim gun on his plane, and he fetched him down with a bang, we like to see anything like that, we got quite excited, worse than being at a football match, we started singing and dancing, and made as much fuss as if the war was over....

Dear mother, did our Bill receive his letter I wrote about a fortnight ago, if so, tell him to hurry up and send me a catapult out so that I can kill a few rats as well as Germans; we have got rat traps set up round about the guns and we catch as many as forty in a night, so you can guess what we have to go through when we are asleep, they are running all over our faces all night, they plague us more than the Germans. I was laying by the gun last night and I was almost afraid to take my head from under my mackintosh.

Your ever loving son
J A Cowley[7]

A young officer's experiences

The son of W W Hutton, agent to Lord Willoughby de Broke, sent an equally vivid description of the life of an officer in October 1915 - equally shocking, if less harrowing.

Dear Mrs Leigh
Thank you so much for the silk socks. It is very kind of you to think of me, and they will be most acceptable.

At present I am not with the guns, as it is my turn to be back with the horses and spare men. We are hidden in a wood, and I have a gypsy tent which consists of sacks, ground sheets and branches. It is not very waterproof but it keeps some of the flies out, which are more trouble than the wet. I have a small table and an armchair with the guns and shall try to get it down here. The table and chair came from a village through which the trenches run, and all the inhabitants have left. The poor beggars had to clear out in twelve hours notice, and left all they possessed behind them, so we get plenty of furniture.

The men sleep in the cellar close to the guns, and the walls leading down to them are rather amusing. One cellar has 'Lyon's Popular Café' on the walls, 'Grill downstairs; the orchestra has been suspended as we have no Germans left and all intelligent Englishmen are at the front. The Company apologise and hope all young men eligible for active service will take note.'

Another one is 'Madame Tussaud's Chamber of Horrors'. It happens to be the ammunition store. Another has 'Please do not tease the animals, buy your nuts at the stall on the left. They are perfectly happy and love their work.'

Last Friday night I was called up to the front line trenches to see a German working party, they were fortifying a house. I got two shells in about one minute straight into them; killed lots of them. But they let us have it back again, they bombarded us with trench mortars first, then rifle grenades with shells joining in. I soon stopped them though. Got the battery pumping big shells back at them and they got the worst of it so it stopped. I cook my own meals; went to the village last night, got some vegetables from the Chateau that is ruined, borrowed some pots and pans from the kitchen. I had soup, beef and vegetables, roast apples and a savoury. My sergeant major presented me with a bottle of liqueur crème de Mandarine, which he got from Bethune.

I am, yours sincerely
W H Hutton[s]

Some of this letter may seem distasteful today, but probably reflects a character better fitted to survive in war than a man more in tune with peacetime sensibilities. He was at the time of writing a second lieutenant in the Royal Field Artillery, promoted further to Captain in December 1916. In March 1917 he received the Military Cross for conspicuous gallantry, won at the battle of the Somme the previous October. In April 1917 he was badly wounded with gunshot wounds in both legs, and it seems likely that he was never able to return to active service again. He presented the book for photographs in December 1917, and it contains photographs of him and of his two younger brothers, Philip, a second lieutenant of the Royal Garrison Artillery, and Sidney, also a second lieutenant in the Warwickshire Yeomanry. Sidney was only seventeen when war broke out, and his father was loathe to lose him. Despite making a good case for keeping him at home to help with the running of Lord Willoughby's 15,600 acre estate and his own 500 acre farm, (a reasonable request when the only help was from

W. H. Hutton, who donated the album for photographs to St Peter's church

a 65 year old retainer), the military authority on the tribunal said "Why should Mr Hutton spoil a glorious record by not giving the lot of them?"

Shell shock

Arguably the most sensitive and revealing letter of those available was sent by Richard Trenfield to his parents, who had been landlords of the Red Lion for some years. Richard, the youngest of the Trenfield sons to serve in the war, was an old Middle School boy (from G W Webb's school) and a member of Kineton church choir. The flat reporting of his letter is totally different from the jingoism of young Mr Hutton.

Last Sunday (May 30th) we had a terrible time in the trenches, we had got a squadron of Scotch Yeomanry in our trenches for just twenty-four hours instruction in trench life. The boys who were very decent fellows indeed had never been under fire before and some of us had been detailed off to instruct them. It was most unfortunate for them being their first day, as we were heavily shelled from twelve o'clock to seven at night. They happened to be big shells, high explosive ones too, most German ones are, but ours are nearly all

William Trenfield, his wife and three of his daughters. The girls are all dressed in their VAD nursing uniform. Strangely, these three girls are not included on the list of nurses at Clarendon Hospital.

shrapnel (not much good). The first dropped about fifty yards behind our trenches, the next about ten yards, and then one dropped about two yards in front, sending clouds of earth all over us. The boys were ordered to clear out our bay (as they had got our range nicely) except the sentries who should have stopped, but the whole lot cleared out so I stopped behind as there was no-one on sentry duty. The next two shells dropped in front but nearer and as I lay on the ground in the trench and felt the ground shake and tremble expecting every minute the front to be blown in something seemed to give me strength and tell me I should be quite safe. Those two shells failed to explode for some reason, and are buried in front of our trench by their own force.

Writing of the military cemetery, he says:

..... It is a beautiful spot on a hillside in a big wood, all among pine trees, and there we lay our poor boys for their last rest. There are quite a lot of little crosses there already and on each mound are planted lilies-of-the-valley.... Last night returning from digging trenches behind the firing line a boy was shot beside me, the bullet hit him in the forehead and came out the back of his head. We bound his head up but could see he was fast going so we got him to a stretcher and four of us carried him some distance to the doctor. He lived until dawn, and then another brave soul passed to its resting place.[9]

Later in the war Richard was invalided out of the 6th Royal Warwickshire's with shell-shock, went to farm in South Africa under a Government scheme for ex-servicemen, and despite his experiences, fought in the second World War also. He died in South Africa.

Two of Richard's brothers also served in the war. Charles Henry Trenfield, the eldest of the three, was a lieutenant in the 6th Dragoon Guards by the end of the war, and Ernest, the middle one, was in the Warwickshire Yeomanry

Charles enlisted as a Private in December 1914, and served with the London Regiment in France until April 1915. He then transferred to the Warwickshire Yeomanry, and in November 1917 took part in the cavalry charge at Huj, where a mounted squadron charged a gun position. Nearly three quarters of them were killed, but Charles, though wounded in the neck, and shaken by the experience of seeing close friends die, survived and was gazetted in April 1918 for "Bravery in the Field" and awarded the Military Medal. For a short while after the war he served as 2nd Lieutenant in the 6th Dragoons.

Ernest received the Military Service Medal for his part in saving the lives of horses on board *HM Transport Wayfarer*, which was torpedoed 60 miles north west of the Scillies. He was one of the fifteen privates who volunteered to go back onto the *Wayfarer*, accompanied by Major Richardson, Lieutenant Yorke, Veterinary Lieutenant Palmer (a Warwick vet, later father-in-law of Colonel John Macghee, the Kineton vet from 1947 to 1984) two

NOTHING is to be written on this side except the date and signature of the sender. Sentences not required may be erased. If anything else is added the post card will be destroyed.

I am quite well.

I have been admitted into hospital

{ *sick* } *and am going on well.*
{ *wounded* } *and hope to be discharged soon.*

I am being sent down to the base.

I have received your { *letter dated* 10/3/17
{ *telegram* ,,
{ *parcel* ,,

Letter follows at first opportunity.

I have received no letter from you

{ *lately*
{ *for a long time.*

Signature } G. Hartless
only }

Date *April 7th 17*

{Postage must be prepaid on any letter or post card addressed to the sender of this card.]

Wt. W3437/693 2924J. 600m. 9/16. C. & Co., Grange Mills, S.W.

A communication from the front. This "official" card had no space for personal messages.

sergeants and a farrier sergeant. The ship was taken in tow, but conditions were very difficult and the yeomen worked up to their waists in water. That night there blew a gale and "no-one slept, soldiers and crew worked under great danger, for any moment the ship might have gone, in fact with six holds out of nine under water it is a marvel she kept afloat at all."[10] In the afternoon of the next day 760 animals were safely landed. Two horses were lost as the result of an accident, and one died of pneumonia.

Ernest Trenfield returned to Kineton, and in February 1927 took over the tenancy and licence of the Red Lion at the death of his father.

Unfortunately I have been unable to trace letters from the front written by any other servicemen, but newspapers and village memories have allowed a brief description of the effects of the war on some other Kineton families. A full alphabetical list of all the known servicemen, with, where possible, their ranks and units, is given in Chapter Eight.

The Askew family

It comes as a considerable shock to hear the names of the three Askew brothers read out first at the beginning of the remembrance service each November. (Names are read in alphabetical order.) The family originally came from Northend, but when the boys were still young they moved to New Farm, Kineton, from where the four boys attended Mr Chandler's school in the village centre, some two miles away. The four brothers all went to war. The eldest, George, enlisted in December 1914 and was sent to France with the Kings Royal Rifles Corps. He was killed in Flanders, at Hooge, and his memorial is on the Menin Gate at Ypres. He, and the other 55000 servicemen who fell in "Flanders fields", and who have no known grave, are to this day remembered at sunset every day, when the traffic of Ypres comes to a standstill and the *Last Post* sounds. Frederick, the second Askew brother to enlist (in August 1916) in the Machine Gun Corps was the luckiest, and returned to Kineton where he died in 1967 at the age of 70 years. The other two boys, Oliver and Horace, enlisted within a few days of each other in 1917, one in the Royal Warwickshire's and the other in the Machine Gun Corps, like Frederick. Both were killed in France, Oliver in March 1918, aged 25, and Horace in December 1918, aged 23. They lie buried only about 5 miles apart at St Souplet and Le Cateau. One of the great tragedies of their story is that their poor mother, by some apparent

Horace Askew, the last of the Askews to die in France. The album page showing his three brothers is on page 4

maladministration, heard about their deaths only within a few days of each other, just before Christmas, 1918, when the war in Europe was officially at an end.

William Barnes

William Barnes, a Kineton policeman, was one of the first villagers to be decorated. He had rejoined the 1st Royal Warwickshire Regiment on mobilisation, and was in France by 13th August 1914. Within a month, as a result of his bravery when he stayed with wounded comrades during

William Barnes in the Stratford Police Force, after the war. He is third from the right in the back row, and his uniform conceals the fact that his left shoulder had been shot away. At this time he was living in Alveston.

heavy shelling of their look-out point, he was awarded the French Medaille Militaire, and the Distinguished Conduct Medal. Bells were rung in his honour when the news was received in Kineton, and when, after he was wounded in April 1915, he returned home to convalesce.

His fellow townsmen took advantage of this occasion to honour him by going en masse to the station to meet him and escort him home. The Kineton Volunteer Corps, under the command of Sergeant Coles, of Southam, formed a guard of honour, lining up on the station as the train steamed in, and then marching on each side of the conveyance to his home, on reaching which he was met by Superintendant Hawkes, head of the constabulary in this division of Warwickshire.[11]

The Fisher family

One family in Kineton sent five sons to fight in the war, an event which merited a telegram from the King, sent on 18th September 1915.

Sir

I have the honour to inform you that the King has heard with much interest that you have at the moment five sons serving in the Army.

I am commanded to express you the King's congratulations, and to assure you that His Majesty much appreciates the spirit of patriotism which prompted this example, in one family, of loyalty and devotion to their Sovereign and Empire.

> *I have the honour to be, Sir,*
> *Your obedient servant,*
> *The Keeper of the Privy Purse.*[12]

Three of the five sons returned from service in Egypt, Palestine, Italy and France, though one had been badly gassed and another had lost a lung; the two elder were killed on successive days. Other telegrams from the King arrived just over a year later, the second of which, on 20th September 1916, read:

TO: J Fisher, Esq, Kineton, Warwickshire

The King and Queen are deeply grieved to hear that you have lost yet another son in the service of his country. Their Majesties offer you their heartfelt sympathy in your fresh sorrow.

> *The Keeper of the Privy Purse*[13]

It was the two eldest sons who lost their lives. Second lieutenant Percy Watkis Fisher, born in December 1881, enlisted in September 1914, and was quickly promoted to Sergeant in the Royal Fusiliers. He was awarded the Distinguished Conduct Medal in July 1916, the interesting citation reading

For conspicuous ability, when his company had attacked and captured an enemy trench, he organised the defence of a flank with great coolness and skill. When a withdrawal was ordered he again displayed great ability, directing the various parties by the bearings of certain stars.[14]

This interest in maps and navigation had begun when he was at school in

Percy Fisher.

Stratford-upon-Avon, at King Edward VI School. After obtaining engineering qualifications he became expert in the telegraphing of maps and was actively engaged in this on the *Times* during the Russian-Japanese War. He also brought out geographical military maps for the War Office. His death, on 12th September 1916, was instantaneous, when he was shot through the heart while out on patrol. He was buried in a small French cemetery at Hebuterne on the Somme that afternoon.

His younger brother, Captain Raymond Wadhams Fisher of the 10th Northumberland Fusiliers, died in action in Salonika just one day later, on 13th September 1916. His career, if anything, was even more extraordinary. Born in February 1883, he, like his brother, was educated at King Edward VI School, Stratford. He first saw service in the Boer War, and joined the Northumberland Fusiliers when war broke out in 1914. He was quickly promoted Captain, and had a machine gun unit under his charge. By the middle of 1916 he had been posted to the general staff, Intelligence Department, in Salonika, probably partly because of his skill with languages - he was fluent in six. There are many stories of his bravery, and of how he

Raymond Fisher

had inspired his troops, but the most amazing part of his life, which had happened before the First World War broke out, was not revealed fully until some years later. Then, in 1936 his family received from the Bulgarian Government the highest honour that they could give for his part in the Bulgarian War. The Bulgarian papers had been glowing in his praise, describing how, in Sofia, he had been known as "The Brave Englishman" and how when the troops returned to Sofia, "Mr Fisher was the special object of the attention of the crowds, who literally heaped flowers upon him[15]" , but it was not until 1936 that the Bulgarians were able to trace the whereabouts of his relations, and restore to them the relics and documents that had been left behind after his death. Among them was the citation and medal of the Soldier's Cross "For Bravery" awarded in 1913.[16]

A sixth son of the family, John Burdon Fisher, the youngest, who was only thirteen at the outbreak of war, stayed in Kineton. Not to be outdone by his brothers, even he played his part by rounding up horses frightened by Zeppelins overhead. He remained in Kineton, running the drapery business in Bridge Street he inherited from his father, until his death in 1986.

The Smith family

In October 1916, the Reverend Franklyn Smith was appointed minister of the Wesleyan chapel, the centre of the Kineton Methodist circuit. He was newly arrived from Barcelona where he had served for twenty years. Two of his sons were serving in the Army, Roderick Franklyn, the elder, being a Captain, and the younger, Douglas George, being a second lieutenant, both in the 6th King's Shropshire Light Infantry. By the time their father left Kineton for his next circuit (in Marazion, Cornwall) both these sons were dead, and their names are remembered proudly on the Kineton Memorial, the village that they could have seen so briefly, and that their parents must have remembered with sadness.

Douglas was the first to be killed, on 16th August, 1917, and he is buried at Dozinghem, not far from Langemark in Belgium. When he joined the Army he was in his second term reading Modern Languages at St Catherine's College, Cambridge, specialising in French and German, but the moment he reached military age he enlisted, and left for France on Christmas Day 1915. In the following June he was awarded the Military Cross for carrying through patrol work while wounded. His knowledge of German made him particularly useful, and coming close to the enemy's lines one night, he overheard a scrap of conversation which led him to conclude that plans were about to be discussed. He lay, it is said, on the top of a wall, and although he had been shot in the arm, he stayed listening until he had heard the plans. The information proved to be of considerable importance and had some influence on the success of later operations. A few days after returning to the front he was wounded a second time, this time in the head. He returned home for several months to recuperate, and went back to France in February 1917. He had been in the trenches on his twenty-first birthday,

The grave of Douglas Smith at Dozinghem.

and on that day was promoted to Second Lieutenant. At his death, the letter to his parents from his commanding officer spoke of his care and handling of his platoon. "His men idolised him".[17]

Roderick was an engineer with a promising career ahead of him, but when war broke out he joined the Seaforth Highlanders, as a private. After ten months in France he obtained a commission in the King's Shropshire, and after a short spell of training in this country, was almost continuously at the front. For distinguished conduct at the attack on Langemark in August 1917, in the action in which his brother received his fatal wounds, he was promoted to Second Lieutenant. In the advance on Cambrai in November 1917 he was awarded the Military Cross, and later he was awarded a bar to it, with the following citation

During an attack it was found that Tanks leading companies of the battalion had veered off and were hotly engaged. Although the trenches had not been fully cleared of the enemy, he volunteered, in spite of heavy fire, to find both companies and Tanks, and succeeded in leading them back, with the result of the complete capture of the objective assigned to the battalion. To this success his courage and initiative greatly contributed.[18]

He fought through the first five days of the German offensive which began on 21st March 1918, and he was killed by a stray machine gun bullet on 28th March 1918, the morning that he returned to the front after two days rest. The fighting was so intense that his grave was not marked. His name is inscribed on the memorial to the fallen at Pozières.[19]

1 *Parish Magazine*, April 1916
2 ibid., July 1916
3 ibid., August 1916
4 ibid., October 1918
5 ibid., September 1915
6 ibid., January 1916
7 ibid., December 1915
8 ibid., October 1915
9 ibid., July 1915
10 **Vice Admiral Coke**, Investigation Report (quoted by Brian Johnson in manuscript for submission to *Regimental Journal*, and lent to author).
11 *Stratford upon Avon Herald*, 1 July 1915
12 Family archive of David Fisher
13 ibid.
14 *London Gazette*, 27 July 1916
15 *Stratford upon Avon Herald*, 29 September 1916
16 ibid., 17 July 1936 and 24 July 1936; *Evesham Journal* 18 July 1936.
17 ibid., 24 August 1917 and *Kingswood School Magazine*, December 1917, page 332
18 *London Gazette*, February 1918
19 *Stratford upon Avon Herald*, 19 April 1918 and *Kingswood School Magazine*, July 1918, page 398

Chapter Eight
Kineton Roll of Honour

Soldiers Who Gave Their Lives

The three soldiers marked by an asterisk have not yet been fully traced. Jan 1998

ASKEW George Edgar

Private   8th Kings Royal Rifle Corps R 8209
Born: 21/1/1891 (Bapt,) Northend   *School:* Kineton
         Son of Joseph and Matilda
Enlisted: December 1914   *Died*: Belgium, Hooge 30/07/15
Memorial: Ypres (Menin gate) panel 51/53
         See p 99

ASKEW Horace Samuel James

Private   62nd Machine Gun Corps 138264
Born: 22/6/1895, Northend
         Son of Joseph and Matilda
Enlisted: May 1917   *Died:* France 03/12/18
Grave: Le Cateau I 38
         See p 99 Died of Broncho-pneumonia

ASKEW Oliver Joseph

Private   2/6th Royal Warwickshire Regiment 25304
Born: 12/3/1893, (Bapt.) Northend
         Son of Joseph and Matilda
Enlisted: July 1917   *Died*: France 20/03/18
Grave: St Souplet, plot3 row B
         See p 99

BALDWIN George Harold

Petty Officer   Royal Navy J/10360 K4 submarine
Born: 1895, Kineton   *Died:* Firth of Forth 31/01/18
         Son of George and Mary
Memorial: K4 submarine memorial, and Plymouth no 27

George Baldwin was to have been married at Christmas 1917, but could not obtain leave. The wedding had been rearranged, but he was killed a week before it took place. Details of the awful accident in which he was killed did not emerge until July 1932. The cruiser *"Fearless"* rammed *K17*, and *K6* and *K4* collided. 115 lives were lost, 55 of them on the K4 which went down with all hands.

George Baldwin in naval uniform

BROWN Jack
Private   11th Royal Warwickshire Regiment 267626
Born: 1898, Little Kineton   *Died:* France 25/04/17
          Son of John and Sarah
Memorial: Arras memorial to the missing bay 3

COLEMAN John George

Corporal   146th Royal Field Artillery, 47310
Born: 1887   *Died:* France 03/05/15
Enlisted: September, 1914
Grave: Bailleul extension, II A 183

Husband of Mrs F M Coleman, this was the first Kineton man to be killed in the Great War.

John Coleman

The grave, as it was first marked, of John Coleman, and his grave today

COLLETT John Ernest William

Lance Corporal 3rd Worcestershire Regiment 13313
Born: 14/6/1896 (Bapt), Kineton School Kineton
          Son of John and Mary Ann, Market Place
Enlisted: Pre May 1915   *Died:* Belgium 11/12/15
Grave: Prowse Point I A 3

COLLINS John Ernest

Rifleman   8th Kings Royal Rifle Corps R8208
Born: 6/10/1895 (Bapt), Kineton
            Son of Joseph and Mary Ann, Bridge St
Enlisted: December, 1914   *Died:* Belgium 22/11/15
Grave: Lijssenthoek II D 1A

Lijssenhoek is one of the largest first world war cemeteries, used by French and British Casualty Clearing Stations throughout the war

* COOPER Albert

Private   *Died:* before 8/11/15

In response to requests printed in several local papers, two people have informed me that the man known as "Albert" Cooper is really Herbert Bernard Cooper of Avon Dassett, and that he worked at the Kennels in Little Kineton. This would appear to be borne out in three ways; first, that Albert Cooper is named on the Roll of Honour given in the Avon Dassett parish council minutes for 1917, though is called Hubert on their War Memorial; second, that Herbert Cooper enlisted in Scarborough, as did fifteen Kineton kennelmen; third, that Herbert Cooper was killed in May 1915.

While this is not proof of his identity, it would seem to be a reasonable assumption.

Probably   Private 18th Hussars 12370 *Died:* Belgium 13/05/15
Memorial: Ypres (Menin Gate) panel 5

ELLICK Charles Moody Matthews

Lance Corporal 10th King's Liverpool (Scottish) 3260(2224)
Born: 26/9/1885, Liverpool
            Son of J H and Lavinia
Enlisted: 1 September 1914   *Died:* France 07/07/15
Grave: Wimereux XII 1

Charles Ellick was the eldest son of the late J H Ellick and Mrs Ellick, of the Royal Institution Liverpool. After a period as a Schoolmaster at his old school, he came to Kineton as secretary to Joshua Fielden, joint master of foxhounds. He is buried in the French part of Wimereux cemetery, near Boulogne, interred in a private grave in the same cemetery as John McCrae, writer of "In Flanders Fields". Although he left a wife who he had married while in Kineton, his property was all left to his mother. She gave the Rolls of Honour hung in Kineton church in his memory.

FISHER Percy Watkis, DCM

2nd lieutenant 22nd Royal Fusiliers 278

Born: 15/12/1881   *School:* KES, Stratford
            Son of Joseph and Mary Ann
Enlisted: August 1914   *Died:* France 12/09/16
Grave: Hebuterne communal cemetery   I A 8
            See p 108

FISHER Raymond Wadhams

Captain   10th Northumberland Fusiliers

Born: 3/7/1883   *School:* KES, Stratford
            Son of Joseph and Mary Ann
Enlisted: 14 August 1914   *Died:* Salonika 13/09/16
Grave: Karasouli, Polycastron   C 508
            See p 108

FREEMAN Albert John

Rifleman   8th Kings Royal Rifle Corps R8207

Born: 1897, Kineton   *School:* Kineton
            Son of William and Agnes
Enlisted: 15 December 1914   *Died:* Belgium 05/07/15
Grave: Ypres (Menin Gate) Memorial   panel 51 or 53

Albert Freeman left for France on 18 May 1915, with his brother. He volunteered for machine gun duty, and was one of the youngest in his platoon. He was killed when a shell burst at the doorway of one of the emplacements, and he and a friend who was killed at the same time were buried together.

FREEMAN George

Private   10th Kings Rifle Brigade S/1548

Born: 4/4/1889 Kineton   *School:* Kineton
            Son of George and Josephine

Enlisted: 5 September 1914   *Died:* France 05/10/15
Grave: Royal Irish Rifles Graveyard, Laventie, France   I H 9

George Freeman was the eldest son of the Gas Works Manager

GARDNER George Frederick
Private   9th Royal Inniskilling Fusiliers 42708
Born: 2/8/1896 (Bapt), Kineton   *School:* Kineton
          Son of Martin and Ada
Enlisted: Pre May 1915   *Died:* France 24/10/18
Grave: Terlincthun British Cemetery VI C 20

Believed to be the youngest son in a family of four brothers. See p 100.
Enlisted as a baker in the Royal Army Service Corps before posting to the
Inniskilling Fusiliers

GARRETT Oliver Thomas
Private   Queen's Own (Royal West Kent) Regiment G/29127
Born: 21/8/1899, Kineton
          Son of Edward and Annie   *Died:* France 01/09/18
Grave: Rancourt   D4

Oliver Garrett was posted to the 1st/20th Battalion London Regiment
towards the end of the war, and it was with them that he lost his life on
the Somme.

GREEN Kelynge
Lance Corporal 11th Royal Warwickshire   17862
Born: 10/9/1893, Kineton   *Died:* France 31/05/18
          Son of Henry and Elizabeth, Bridge St
Grave: Chambrecy   IV C 4

HARTLESS Geoffrey
Private   Royal Fusiliers (2nd/2nd London) 232514(5554)
Born: 21/8/1895
          Son of Samuel and Annie
Enlisted: August 1916   *Died:* France 14/05/17
Memorial: Arras memorial bay 9

Geoffrey Hartless was one of the First team, Lewis Gun section. He was killed only about two weeks after arriving at the front. See p 114

Geoffrey Hartless.

The medals received by the family of Geoffrey Hartless after his death. Geoffrey was too young to serve early in the war, and so did not receive the "Mons" star or the 1914-15 Star. The brass plaque was sent to the next of kin of those who were killed, together with a scroll and a letter from the King.

HORSLEY Joseph W

Lance corporal 9th Royal Sussex Regiment 4198
Born: 13/1/1892 (Bapt), Kineton
　　　　Son of Abraham and Emma　　　*Died:* Belgium 21/06/17
Grave: Oxford rd IV F 2

When a boy, Joseph Horsley worked in Lord Willoughby de Broke's gardens at Woodley House. He left there to go to the Duke of Norfolk's gardens at Arundel Castle from where he enlisted. He was wounded twice, and gassed before his death in 1917.

HUDSON Charles Albert

Sergeant　　　　1st Warwickshire Yeomanry 1174
Born: Longborough, Gloucestershire
　　　　Son of John and Ann
Enlisted: September 1914　　　　*Died:* Egypt 10/08/16
Grave: Kantara

Charles Hudson resided at Kineton for 20 years and was a servant of Lord Willoughby de Broke. He was a crack shot (Prize, Bisley, 1912) in the Warwickshire Yeomanry for nine years, and was discharged in 1914. At the outbreak of war he re-enlisted, and mobilised at Warwick with B squadron under Major Bernard Granville of Wellesbourne. He was seriously wounded, and later died of his wounds, after holding out against Turkish and German attacks when sent to reinforce the Auckland Rifles (a New Zealand battalion).

Charles Hudson

* KEYTE William
Private

The Commonwealth War Graves Commission registers have three men by the name of William Keyte listed as killed. None of the three has any known connection with Kineton, but for the sake of completeness the three are listed briefly

a) 1st Grenadier Guards 22880   *Died:* 21/11/16,
Born and enlisted: Nottingham Memorial to the missing, Thiepval, panel 8D

b) 4th King's (Liverpool) Regiment 109379   *Died:* 13/10/18
At time of death wife living in Prestwich, Manchester.
Grave: Rocquigny-Equancourt XII B2

c) 4th Worcestershire Regiment 13101 *Died:* 6/5/15
An Alcester man
Memorial: Helles memorial to the missing, Turkey

There is, however, a tenuous link between Kineton and the last soldier of these three. Though born in Alcester, William Keyte enlisted in Redditch, and he was a needle maker. In the introduction to her husband's book *The Passing Years* (Constable, 1924) Lady Willoughby de Broke writes ".....the needlemakers of Redditch who on Sundays turned up 'en masse' at the meets, prepared to run all day with the hounds....wrote tributes..." I have been unable to verify the connection.

LOUCH Frank
Private   1/6th Royal Warwickshire Regiment 5226
Born: 30/1/1884 (Bapt), Holy Trinity, Stratford-on-Avon
          Son of John and Caroline   *Died:* France 18/08/16
Memorial: Thiepval pier 9A

MIZEN William John
Sapper 92nd Royal Engineers 108948
Born: 1883   Son of Joseph and Mercey
Enlisted: 22 March 1916   *Died:* France 16/06/18
Grave: Ribemont extension IV G 8

William Mizen was in the Royal Engineers for 12 years before the outbreak of the First World War. He rejoined in March 1916, and before he was sent to France on 15 October 1916, married Lottie Freeman, a teacher at Kineton weekday and Sunday school. He was invalided home in February 1917 and returned to France fourteen months later, in April 1918. He was killed by a shell in action in June of that year.

MULLIS Herbert George
Private   9th Royal Warwickshire Regiment 13381
Born: Kineton   *Died:* Mesopotamia 18/04/16
Grave: Chalelah, Mesopotamia

PADBURY Sam
Private   2nd Royal Warwickshire Regiment 21915
Born: 10/9/87 (Bapt), Kineton
          Son of Thomas and Hannah   *Died:* France 04/05/17
Memorial: Arras memorial   bay 3

Sam Padbury was one of over 250 casualties of the unsuccessful action at Mory Copse, the aim of which was to support an attack by the Anzac Corps on the Hindenburg line. The failure of the action was put down to a heavy barrage and uncut belt of wire; a maze of dug-outs; and poor communications compounded by bad visibility, a broken signalling lamp and the death from shell shock of the two communication pigeons.

PHILPOT Henry John
Private   7th South Staffordshire 10941
Born: 4/7/1890 (Bapt), Kineton
          Son of George and Edith
Enlisted: August 1914   *Died:* Dardenelles 09/08/15
Memorial: Helles memorial, Turkey

PLUMMER George Frederick
Sergeant   1st Warwickshire Yeomanry 310254(867)
Born: 25/8/1882 (Bapt), Kineton   *School:* Kineton
          Son of Frederick and Hannah
Enlisted: 4 August 1914   Died   Palestine 08/11/17
Grave: Gaza War Cemetery   XIX C 1

George Plummer had been in the Yeomanry since May 1901 and was called up at the outbreak of war. He served in Egypt for 2 years and had not been home for 20 months before he was killed. The Sinai Desert campaign included the battles of Katia, Rafu, Beersheba and the three battles of Gaza. Sergeant Plummer took part in the famous charge at Huj, wielding his sword alongside Sergeant L J Lambert and Private S Capes, both from the Kineton area. The Commanding Officer was Captain Rudolph Valentine, a member of the Warwickshire hunt. The two sergeants were recommended for awards for great gallantry. Both were killed.

George Plummer, in a characteristic pose.

PRICKETT Albert Frederick

Private   Royal Army Service Corps (38th div Mech Trans) M2/188787
Born: 25/10/1889 (Bapt), Kineton   *School:* Kineton
          Son of William and Selina
Enlisted: Pre May 1915   *Died:* France 14/02/19
Grave: Doullens Cemetery no 2   II E 21

Originally in the Royal Warwickshire Regiment, Albert Prickett was seriously gassed in 1915. He died of disease in hospital in Doullens after the end of the war. Doullens was the head quarters of Marshall Foch throughout the war, and the scene of the 1918 conference at which Marshall Foch assumed command of the Allied forces.

ROBERTS William

Private   2nd Ox and Bucks Light Infantry 9038
Born: Islington   *Died:* France 15/03/16
Grave: Tranchee de Mecknes A 2

William Roberts died at his post while on sentry duty in the firing line. A German trench mortar burst very close to him and he was killed instantly. Tranchée de Mecknes cemetery was begun by the French troups and named after the Arab town from which they had come. Taken over by the British in 1916, it is 1200 yards from the nearest road.
See p 119

ROUSE Denis Charles

Private   50th Machine Gun Corps 108427
Born: 11/11/1898 (Bapt), Kineton France
          Son of Arthur and Frances   *Died:* Trelon, France 18/08/18
Grave: Glageon   A 1

Denis Rouse died in a Prisoner of War hospital. It is believed that he was made to carry shells to the German lines, and died in hospital of starvation.

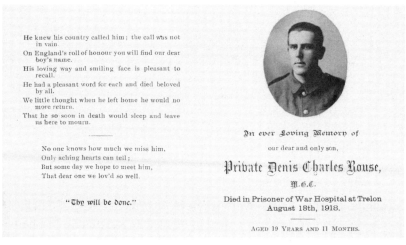

The memorial card for Denis Rouse, prepared by his grieving parents

SMITH Douglas George   MC
Lieutenant   6th Kings Shropshire Light Infantry
Born: 1886   Son of Franklyn George and Marie Laurence
Enlisted: September 1917   *Died:* France 16/08/17
Grave: Dozingen   III I 7

SMITH Roderic Franklyn M C & bar
Captain   6th Kings Shropshire Light Infantry
Born: 1882   Son of Franklyn George and Marie Laurence
Enlisted: September 1914   *Died:* France 28/03/18
Memorial: Pozieres   panel 60

STRATFORD William
Private   2nd Kings Royal rifle Brigade S/6606
Born: 25/11/1894 (Bapt),Binton
            Son of Samuel and Harriet   *Died:* Belgium 25/09/15
Memorial: Ploegsteert   panel 10

William Stratford was born in Binton and is also commemorated on the War Memorial in Binton churchyard. He was an employee of the Stratford and Midland Junction Railway, and in Kineton worked as a porter at the station. He was also a well-known member of the St Peter's church choir. He was first wounded in May 1915, when the explosion of a shell knocked him down, burning his face and badly damaging one eye and his right arm.

* TAYLOR John
Private   Royal Field Artillery
Born: 1898   *Died:* September 1917
Enlisted: 1915

TIPPING Roland Walter
Private   15th Royal Warwickshire Regiment 242900
Born: 16/7/1893 (Bapt), Kineton   Son of Walter and
Enlisted: After March 1916   *Died:* France 24/08/18
Grave: Bagneux   IV G 9

Roland Tipping of Pittern Hill, Kineton, enlisted in the Warwickshire

Yeomanry, no 1663, on 27 February 1910. He was discharged after four years, and at the outbreak of war did not rejoin. Following the introduction of conscription in 1916, he applied for exemption from call up because his father was stone deaf and needed his youngest son both to help on the 177-acre farm, and to interpret for him in deaf and dumb language at stock sales and at market. The appeal was dismissed in April 1916, and he joined the Royal Warwickshire Regiment as a signaller. It is likely that he died on the Somme at no 29 Casualty Clearing Station from wounds received in what has been described as "one of the most successful attacks the 15th battalion ever made"(*The 15th Battalion Royal Warwickshire Regiment in the Great War* by Major C A Bill). It was an action in which few British were killed or wounded, but which advanced the front well over two miles, with the capture of over 200 German prisoners and a large amount of artillery and equipment. At the time of his death his wife and young son lived in Alcester.

WHEILDON John

Sergeant   1st Warwickshire Yeomanry 1368(310360)
Born: 15/2/1889, Gaydon   Son of John and Margaret
Enlisted: 14 August 1914   *Died:* Egypt 19/04/17
Memorial: Jerusalem

John Wheildon enlisted on 10 May 1907, from Gaydon, and was called up the day after war was declared. He went to Gallipoli and was wounded at Chocolate Hill in August 1915. He was wounded again at the battle of Romani (8 August 1916), before being killed in action at the first battle of Gaza. His commanding officer, Captain Valentine, commended him as a "first-class horseman, a man invaluable with awkward remounts."

WILKINS Victor J

Sapper   4th Field squadron, Royal Engineers 288525
Born: 29/5/98 (Bapt), Kineton   Son of Ernest and Emily
Enlisted: May, 1917   *Died:* Kantara, Egypt 03/12/18
Grave: Kantara   F 196

Mr and Mrs Wilkins of the Post Office, Kineton, were notified of the dangerous illness of their second son, Victor, on 23 November 1918. On 3 December he died of malaria at the Stationary Hospital, Kantara.

WILSON Arthur
Bombadier   92nd battery Royal Field Artillery 70199
Born: 1894   *Died:* Dardenelles 30/07/15
Grave: Lancashire landing   E 64
          See p 125

Soldiers Who Returned

Information for this list, which is as complete as possible, has been drawn from many sources, including family memory. There are some anomalies, and, I am sure, some omissions. The author would be very pleased to hear from anyone who could add details or correct errors.

ASKEW Frederick
Private   Machine Gun Corps
Born: 23/5/1897 (Bapt.) Northend
Enlisted: Aug 1916   *Died:* 1967
          See also p 85

BAKER Michael
Enlisted: Pre 8/1/15

BALDWIN Jack
Royal Navy   *Enlisted:* 1914

BALDWIN William Leonard
Royal Navy   *Enlisted:* Nov 1915

BANCROFT Charles Lewis
Lieut.   9th, later 3rd, Royal Warwickshire
Born: 10/7/1896 (Bapt), Kineton
          Attended Warwick School. Second son of Charles Bancroft, Chemist.
          Enlisted by June 1915. Joined the 9th Royal Warwickshire's as they came
          off the peninsula, and after a month in Egypt, joined General Gorridge's
          relief force for Kut. Received a gun shot wound in left lung on 18 April
          1916 and after a month in Alexandria hospital sent home on sick leave.
          Only returned to light duties. After the War obtained a BA at Cambridge

University, and a Diploma in Forestry, and in 1921 was appointed Assistant Conservator of Forests in British East Africa.

BANCROFT Geoffrey Houlden
Born: 27/9/1894 (Bapt), Kineton

Eldest son of Charles Bancroft, Chemist   Probably attended Warwick School. Pharmaceutical student and bank agent. Applied for exemption in September 1916, and in February 1917 was sent for a medical, despite his widowed mother's plea to the tribunal that he was essential to the running of the family pharmacy. He passed his medical as Grade 1, and therefore joined up early in 1918.

BANCROFT Philip Laurence
2nd lieut.   4th Royal Warwickshire, prev. Artists Rifles.
Born: 23/2/1898 (Bapt), Kineton   *Enlisted:* 19/09/16

Youngest son of Charles Bancroft, Chemist. Attended Warwick School.

BARNES William John DCM, MM
Sergeant   1st Royal Warwickshire   9728
Born: 1886   *Enlisted:* 13/08/14   *Died:* Alveston 1940

BASTIN C

BATCHELOR Arthur
Private   2/4th Ox and Bucks L I   34369

BATCHELOR George
Private Dorsets, or RFA
Born: 1893, Kineton   *Enlisted:* Pre September 1917

BATCHELOR William George
Born: 20/4/1881 (Bapt), Kineton

BATES George DSM
Bombadier   R.F.A
School: Kineton   *Enlisted:* 1912

Awarded the DSM for an act of Bravery on 21 March 1918, near St

Emilie. He showed unflinching courage in the face of a hail of bullets.

BATES George Snr

BATES J

BAYLISS A(lbert)

BAYLISS B

BEASLEY T W
Sapper   Royal Engineers   171591

Employee of Stratford and Midland Junction Railway

BENBOW Alfred
Enlisted: Pre 8/1/15

BLUNT George R
Gunner   56th London/281st brigade R F A   2086
Born: 24/9/1883 (Bapt), Kineton

BLUNT Joseph Henry
Private   Royal Warwickshire
Born: 12/12/1880 (Bapt), Kineton   *School:* Kineton
Enlisted: Pre September 1914

BOULTON William G
Corporal

Torpedoed on Allen Lines' *'Hesperian'* off Fastnet in 1915, and taken prisoner of war in March 1918. As prisoner he was sent back to the lines under British fire, and employed in making roads and light railways. For two months he and his fellow prisoners were given no shelter, not allowed to wash or shave, and the food was very bad.

BRADLEY William E
Enlisted: Pre 8/1/15
Worked in the Estate Office of Lord Willoughby de Broke, and lost the sight of his left eye in 1917

BRAND Humphrey Randolph
Sub lieut   Royal Navy

On *H.M.S Indomitable* in the North Sea. He took part in the battle between Vice-Admiral Sir David Beatty's squadron and German battle cruisers under General Hiffer. The British admiral signalled 'Well done *Indomitable* owing to the remarkable speed she attained. After the attack the *Indomitable* towed the *Lion* back.

BRATT Sidney
Air Mechanic   1st Class   RAF 333700
Born: 30/9/1894 (Bapt), Kineton

BRETHERICK G W
Royal Navy   *School:* Kineton
Enlisted: Pre May 1915

First post as Boy Telegraphist, *HMS Vernon*, later *HMS Nottingham*.

BROWN Harry

BUBB John William MM
Sergeant   Royal Warwickshire
Born: 1885, Kineton   *Died:* 10/06/33, Kineton

BURROWS Henry
Royal Army Medical Corps   *School:* Kineton
Enlisted: Pre May 1915

BURTON Charles
9th Worcester   *School:* Kineton
Enlisted: Pre 8/1/15

CAREW Jasper

CHARLTON Godfrey Cyril
Sergeant   29th div A.S C
Enlisted: November 1914

CLIFTON Edward Arthur
Reporter on the *Rugby Advertiser.* Given temporary exemption by the tribunal until July 1916.

COLLETT George Henry
Baker   ASC, then 7th Field Battery Company
Born: 13/7/1890 (Bapt), Kineton   *School:* Kineton
Enlisted: Pre September 1917

COLLINS Frederick
Gunner   Royal Field Artillery
Born: 13/4/1888 (Bapt), Kineton   *School:* Kineton
Enlisted: Pre November 1915

COLLINS Jo
Worcestershire
Born: 10/7/1898 (Bapt), Kineton   *Enlisted:* Pre 24/11/15

COLLINS Tom Albert
Private   Warwickshire Yeomanry
Born: 6/6/1890 (Bapt), Kineton   *School:* Kineton
Enlisted: Pre Pre May 1915

COLLINS W H

COOPER W
Born: 17/8/1879 (Bapt), Kineton   *Enlisted:* Pre 8/1/15

COURT Francis J
South Wales Borderers
Enlisted: Pre 24/11/16

COURTNEY Henry
Born: 1881   *Died:* Kineton 22/04/52

COWLEY John Arthur
Born: 1887, Kineton   *Died:* Kineton 26/12/54
Enlisted: Pre September 1914

COWLEY John H
Bombadier   Royal Field Artillery
Born: 5/6/1904 (Bapt), Kineton   *School:* Kineton
Enlisted: Pre May 1915

COWLEY Robert
Born: 16/5/1897 (Bapt), Kineton

COWLEY William
Born: 2/9/1889 (Bapt), Kineton

COX John Isaac
Enlisted: Pre 8/1/15

CRONIN John C
Warwickshire Yeomanry

CRONIN Thomas
Sergeant Major   Warwickshire Yeomanry

CUTHBERT Ernest
Enlisted: Pre September 1914

DARLOW Joseph Richard
Gunner   R.F.A
Born: 19/4/1895   *Enlisted:* Pre 25/9/14

DARLOW Sam
Enlisted: Pre 8/1/15

DOWNES J
Born: Chipping Norton?

DUCKETT Frank William
Born: 25/4/1884 (Bapt), Kineton   *Died:* Kineton 21/12/60

Master Tailor, and Prudential agent. Sent into the army in November 1918 despite his appeal that he had only one eye and a plea by the Prudential that his business was essential to Kineton.

DUCKETT Harry E
Royal Navy
Born: 27/8/1893 (Bapt), Kineton   *Enlisted:* Pre 8/1/15

DUCKETT John George
Driver 661 Company A S C 325844
Born: 7/2/1878, Kineton

Until September 1916 was tenant of Bloxham's Farm, Chadshunt, but was unable to find another farm. Applied to delay his call up in order to complete a contract to deliver two hayricks for the Government. This was not allowed at appeal in March 1917.

DURHAM David

EDDEN Harry
Born: 15/5/1895 (Bapt), Kineton

EDDEN W E
WheelerNo1 Company A.S.C T4/094066
Born: 12/4/1896 (Bapt) Kineton   *Enlisted:* April 1915
Died: 19/07/55, Kineton

EDDEN W J
RAF 294562

EDDEN Walter Joseph
Wheelwright Army Service Corps
Born: 1/7/1882 (Bapt), Kineton   *School:* Kineton
Enlisted: Pre May 1915

EDDEN Wilfred

EDDEN William

EDEN George
Private Royal Berkshire
Born: 1/11/1891 (Bapt) Kineton   *School:* Kineton
Enlisted: Pre May 1915   *Discharged:* June 1917

EDEN Harry
Private Royal Berkshire
School: Kineton   *Enlisted:* Pre May 1915

Received his discharge in 1917, having been badly wounded in the foot. Believed to have been treated and operated on at Clarendon Hospital.

EDKINS John Stephen
Enlisted: Pre 8/1/15

EDWARDS Alfred
Died: 17/1/45, Banbury
Son of Herbert

EDWARDS Herbert
Born: 1876   *Died:* 09/03/49

Granted exemption on various occasions to allow him to continue work at the kennels until February 1918.

EDWARDS Irving
Born: 4/8/1876

Proprietor of the Swan Inn. Applied successfully for exemption from service in July 1916. He claimed to be providing stabling at the Inn for 30 horses, with no help, though it is now difficult to see how so many horses could ever have been accommodated on the premises. The inn was inspected for billeting purposes in mid-1917 and said to be suitable for 20 horses and 50 men. His first appeal described his wife as being in poor health and unable to manage the Inn so that Irving Edwards felt his living would be sacrificed if he were called up. In November 1916, by which time he was said to be working full-time on the land as well as managing the Inn, he was called for a medical, and given exemption until those in category C3 were needed.   The result of this medical was questioned, and he went into the forces in July 1917

FIELD Percy Thomas
Warwickshire Yeomanry
Born: 1890, Butlers Marston   *Died:* 1970

One of the fifteen stablemen. See p 00. Later Butler to Lord Willoughby. Left Kineton between the wars.

FIELDEN Anthony
Captain 10th Hussars
Born: 30/3/1886   *Died:* 26/8/1972

Nephew of Joshua and Dora Fielden. Enlisted in 1914, after his wedding to Miss Phoebe Brand at Glynde Place in July 1914. Badly wounded in November 1914, and was still reported incapacitated in July 1915. It was not until February 1916 that he was sufficiently recovered to be able to return to France, as Brigade Major of the 6th and 8th Cavalry brigades.

FIELDEN Lionel
Originally Artists Rifles, later (1915-1919) Royal Garrison Artillery
Enlisted: Pre 8/1/15

Educated at Eton and Brasenose, Oxford.   Became Assistant High Commissioner in the Levant in 1923, and joined the BBC in 1927. After becoming the controller of Broadcasting in India, in 1940 he was appointed Indian Editor of the BBC, and Staff Editor at the Observer in 1942. He died in Lucca, 1/6/74.

FISHER Archibald Rooke
Trooper   Warwickshire Yeomanry, later 10th Hussars
Born: 1897   *Died:* 03/07/46

Served in Palestine and Gibraltar

FISHER Joseph
Warwickshire Yeomanry, later South Staffordshire
Born: 1898   *Died:* 1970

Served in France and Italy

FISHER Reginald
Lieut   10th Northumberland fusiliers, later Royal Welch Fusiliers
Born: 1891   *Died:* 1969

Joined the 19th Alberta Dragoons in Edmonton, Canada at the outbreak
of war, and left for special service on 27 August, 1914. Very badly
wounded in November 1917, and mentioned in Despatches. Served in
Egypt and Palestine.
These three were half brothers of the two elder Fisher sons who were
killed. See p 89

FRANKLIN William H

FREEMAN Bert
Born: 19/1/1893 (Bapt), Kineton

A garage hand at Hiatt's Garage, he was at first given exemption from
service. In August 1916 this exemption was withdrawn, largely, as
Joshua Fielden stated, because 'there was no-one with cars in Kineton
now'.

FREEMAN Charles
Kings Royal Rifles
Born: 17/6/1894 (Bapt),Kineton   *School:* Kineton
Enlisted: Pre May 1915   *Died:* 10/01/65, Kineton

FREEMAN Ernest C
Captain Irish Guards, later 8th Hampshire
Born: 1888, Kineton   *School:* Kineton
Enlisted: Pre May 1915

First went to France in 1914, and wounded at Laventie in November
1915 He was gazetted 2nd lieut. with the Royal Warwickshire Regiment

in March 1917 and went with the Egyptian Expeditionary Force attached
to the 8th Hampshire Regiment in July 1917. Wounded in Palestine,
promoted to Captain in September 1918, and mentioned in Despatches.
In the Birthday Honours list, June 1919. Returned to Kineton, wounded,
in January 1919.

FREEMAN Harry W
Sergeant   16th Royal Warwickshire, (3rd Birmingham) 21018
Born: 29/3/1880 (Bapt), Kineton

Applied for exemption from service in June 1916, on the grounds that his
father, painter and decorator of Coffee House, Kineton, was unable to
manage the business on his own. He was only granted a month's grace,
and enlisted on 15/08/16. He rose steadily through the ranks, first
serving in France, where he returned after a spell in Italy.

FREEMAN Thomas
Born: 20/12/1891 (Bapt), Kineton

GARDNER Fritz MC
Captain   Royal Engineer

Enlisted in 1915, and served in France with the Signal Service. Awarded
the Military Cross in May 1916, and mentioned in Despatches on 31 May
1916 and 14 December 1917. He lived in the farm adjacent to Clarendon
House, which he lent as an extension to the hospital in June 1916.

GARDNER Charles
Royal Marines
Born: 2/8/1896 (Bapt), Kineton
See W H Gardner, below.

GARDNER Martin Blackett
Private   18th Hussars
Born: 6/3/1891 (Bapt), Kineton   *School:* Kineton
Enlisted: Pre May 1915
See W H Gardner, below.

GARDNER William Henry MM
Corporal   Royal Marines
Born: 6/11/1892 (Bapt)   *School:* Kineton
Enlisted: Pre May 1915

The three Gardners are all probably the same family, sons of "Mac" Gardner, and brothers of George Frederick Gardner, who lost his life. See p 90

GARRETT Arthur Sidney MM
Private 1/4th Ox and Bucks L I
Born: 21/1/1894 (Bapt), Kineton   *School:* Kineton
Enlisted: Pre May 1915

In peacetime a scout patrol leader, he enlisted 4 August 1914, and was awarded the Military Medal for service in Italy.

GARRETT Ernest
Private   18th Hussars
School: Kineton   *Enlisted:* Pre May 1915

GARRETT Fred

GARRETT Percy James
Born: 26/5/1901 (Bapt), Kineton

GASKELL Francis Roy
Wounded: April 1918

GEDEN Arthur Bruce MC
Lieut   Royal Navy
Born: 11/8/1891, Kineton   *School:* Kineton
Enlisted: Pre May 1915

The second son joined the naval division at the beginning of the war, and fought from beginning to end of the Gallipoli campaign. After typhoid fever brought him home in 1916, he returned to France where he was awarded the Military Medal for gallantry in leading his men. He was badly wounded in 1917, so much so that the Parish magazine (mistakenly!) reported his death in September 1917.

GEDEN George
New Zealand Expeditionary Force
School: Kineton   *Enlisted:* Pre May 1915

The elder brother of Arthur, he joined the expeditionary force in New Zealand, and met up with his brother at Port Said in 1916. Later he was heavily gassed at Messines Ridge, and treated in London

GIBBINS Albert
Born: 7/12/01, Radway

One of the fifteen stablemen. See p 10

GODMAN John
(eventually) Lt Colonel   15th Hussars
Born: 1886.

A nephew of Lord Willoughby de Broke. Posted missing April 1918.

GOLBY Tom
Transport Motor Driver
Born: 1886, Kineton   *School:* Kineton
Enlisted: Pre May 1915

GOLBY William
Born: 2/4/1893 (Bapt), Kineton

GOLDER H
Enlisted: Pre 8/1/15

GOODENOUGH Leonard W V
Chaplain   Warwickshire Yeomanry

Appointed chaplain to the Yeomanry in 1908. He was mobilised at Warwick on 4 August 1914, and became chaplain to the brigade at Matruh in December 1915. He was in the successful actions in the Senussi campaign. He died at Sittingbourne, Kent in 1920.

GREEN Harry Holtom
Private
Born: 1/10/1897, Kineton

GREEN Harry
Driver   17th div R.F.A 1150
Born: 1/7/1894 (Bapt), Kineton.   *School:* Kineton
Enlisted: Pre May 1915 Prisoner-of-war, returned to Kineton in 1919

GREEN John W
Private 3/7th Royal Warwickshire
Born: September 1895, Kineton

GREEN Wesley
Private   Worcestershire
School: Kineton   *Enlisted:* Pre May 1915

GRIMES Samuel Percy
Born: 9/5/1885

In the employ of Lionel Charles Hiatt, garage owner and ironmonger, who was away on active service.   Sam Grimes applied successfully for exemption in June 1916, again in October, and again in March 1917, but at his last appearance at the appeal tribunal, despite a plea by Florence Hiatt that his call up would oblige her to close down the business, it was politely suggested that within two months he should enlist - which he did.

GRIMSHAW Sam

HANBURY Basil
Lieut Colonel
Born: 1862   *Died:* 20/12/33, Kineton

HANBURY Harold
2nd Lieut   Warwickshire Yeomanry

Born in 18 June 1898, the only son of Patience and Basil Hanbury. After the war he took his degree at Brasenose College, Oxford, and an academic career eventually led to him becoming Vinerian Professor of English Law at the University of Oxford in 1949

HANCOCK Alfred George
Trooper   Warwickshire Yeomanry   169982
Born: 11/7/1897 (Bapt), Kineton.   *Enlisted:* 08/07/15

Saw active service in Egypt, from November 1915 to May 1918. He was torpedoed in the Mediterranean on his way home from Egypt, on the '*Leasowe Castle*' and then served in France.

HANCOCK C
Driver   A S C Motor Transport

Rejected at both Longmoor, Hampshire in September 1914, and in Bath in February 1916, it was 10/12/17 before he saw active service in Italy

HANCOCK Frederick John
Private 2/5th Gloucestershire 12720
Born: 6/1/1895 (Bapt), Kineton.   *Enlisted:* September 1914

Wounded twice in 1916. Served mostly in France.

HANCOCK Henry Jesse
Private   2nd Devonshire 70455
Born: 30/4/1899 (Bapt), Kineton.   *Enlisted:* 09/04/17

Sent abroad in April 1918. Less than two months later he was taken prisoner of war, and returned home at the beginning of 1919.

HANCOCK Montague
Born: 1899

HANCOX Charles

HANCOX George

HANCOX Jack
Private   9th Gloucestershire
School: Kineton   *Enlisted:* Pre May 1915

HANCOX Jesse
Returned to Kineton at the beginning of 1919, having been a prisoner of war.

HARDIMAN George William
Stud groom to Mrs Gaskell of Diana Lodge. Because she had already lost so many staff, his claim for exemption was at first accepted, and even extended in February 1917 as he had sole care of six horses, one of which was destined for the army. His period of exemption ran out at the end of March 1917.

HARRIS Ted

HARRIS William Henry
Born: 5/2/1875 (Bapt), Kineton

HARTLESS William John
Gloucestershire, later Machine Gun Corps
Enlisted: 13/05/15
Brother of Geoffrey Hartless. See p 91

HAWKINS Geoffrey
Born: 15/2/1901 (Bapt), Kineton

HAWKINS Raymond John
Royal Army Medical Corps
Born: 10/6/99 (Bapt), Kineton   *Enlisted:* Pre7/9/17

HAZELWOOD H

HIATT Lionel C
Enlisted: Pre June 1916

HITCHINS W
Enlisted: September 1914

HOARE Charles

HUGHES George

HUGHES Harry
Born: 1899, Ledbury   *Enlisted:* Pre12/10/17

HUNT George
Private   Grenadier Guards
Born: 1886, Kineton   *School:* Kineton
Enlisted: Pre May 1915

HUNT William Oliver
Rough Rider   Army Service Corps
Born: 8/11/1891 (Bapt), Kineton   *School:*   Kineton
Enlisted: Pre May 1915

HUTTON Philip
2nd Lieut   Royal Garrison Artillery
Born: 9/11/1896 (Bapt), Kineton   *Enlisted:* Pre June 1916

Second son of W W Hutton, agent to Lord Willoughby de Broke. Served as a dispatch rider in France.

HUTTON Sidney
2nd lieut   Warwickshire Yeomanry
Born: 3/12/1897 (Bapt), Kineton

Youngest son of W W Hutton.

HUTTON William Hugh MC
Captain Royal Field Artillery
Born: 23/10/1892 (Bapt), Kineton   *Enlisted:* before 9/10/14.

IVENS Albert
Private   1st Royal Warwickshire
Born: 4/3/1894 (Bapt), Kineton   *School:* Kineton
Enlisted: September 1914

> Son of Mr Ivins of the Rose and Crown. Wounded in October 1914 having come through the battle of Mons unscathed, despite fighting there for 72 hours non-stop.

IVENS Harry
Botha's Horse
School: Kineton   *Enlisted:* Pre May 1915

IVENS Walter
Ox and Bucks L I
Born: 7/1/1898 (Bapt), Kineton   *School:* Kineton
Enlisted: September 1914

KIRTLAND Cecil
Born: 1885, Kineton

LANGLEY Fred W

LANGLEY Harry
Enlisted: Pre 8/1/15

LEWIS Frederick James
Born: 1890, Kineton

> Dairyman of Green Farm, and previously a baker. Because his employer, Mr J W Evans, was needed to serve as a vet, his application for exemption in June 1916 was accepted temporarily, but his exemption was not renewed at his re-appearance in September. He appealed, fully supported by his employer, who stated that Lewis was doing the work of the three men who had previously been employed for milking, and that although labour needs had undoubtedly been reduced by the acquisition of a milking machine, his wife was too fully occupied in the dairy to be expected to help with the milking also. The herd supplied Clarendon

Hospital with milk, and because of this he was allowed exemption indefinitely in January 1917. He enlisted at some time after this date.

LITTLEWORTH Alfred

Applied for exemption in May 1916. At this time he was a whipper-in at the kennels, and his application was fully endorsed by Joshua Fielden, who stated that 15 men had gone from the kennels, and that he was left only with five old men to look after the horses, two whippers-in, a huntsman, a kennel-man and a boy. As the other whipper-in was a single man keen to join up, and Alfred Littleworth a married man with a family, Joshua Fielden felt justified in asking to keep him. He was given a month to see if the other whipper-in would be accepted into the army, which in fact he was, but Littleworth also enlisted.

LOUCH Peter

LOVEBAND Lockfort or Rockfort
Royal Navy

Distant relation of the Vicar, W H B Yerburgh

LOVEBAND Gerald
Enlisted: Pre 8/1/15

Distant relation of the Vicar, W H B Yerburgh

LOVESAY Charles
Born: Gaydon

MARSHALL R
Enlisted: Pre 8/1/15

MULLIS Charles Henry
Born: 12/8/1875, Kineton

Described as grocer's porter for J Griffin of Bridge Street before becoming a hay-cutter and presser for G E Boulton at Battle Farm, he was given exemption until October 1916 for farm work. In March 1917, by which time he was working as a corn shifter for Mr Rouse, his application was refused, and he went into the army.

MULLIS Edward

MULLIS James Walter
Born: 1881, Kineton

The only man employed at Brooklands Farm by Mr Esmy Griffin, he was exempted from service in June 1916, but nevertheless enlisted.

MUSTO Edward
Private   6th Warwick Infantry Brigade
School: Kineton   *Enlisted:* November 1914

Son of one of Lord Willoughby de Broke's gardeners, Edward Musto was rejected by the Army because of hammer toe. Such was his enthusiasm to serve, though, that he went to Birmingham for an operation on his toe, and six weeks later, in November 1914, was accepted into the forces.

NEWBOLD Joe

Applied, unsuccessfully, for exemption in July 1916

OLDHAM J Charles
Private   1st Ox and Bucks L I   204641
Enlisted: 07/09/16   *Died:* Kineton, aged 87

Left Cosham, Portsmouth, on 12 December 1917 for service in India.

OLDMEADOW Lloyd John Hollis
Captain Royal Army Medical Corps

Joined up in November 1915, and served in England and France, though chiefly in Dartford, Kent, until November 1917, when he returned to Kineton and became surgeon to Kineton VAD hospital.

PARGETER Walter
Died: 24/11/1957, aged 73, Kineton

PAYNE John

POWELL Arthur
Private   Royal Berkshire   28510

 Brother-in-law of William Roberts, see p 96

POWELL John

PRICE Geoffrey
Lieut   Royal Army Medical Corps

 Enlisted at the beginning of September 1917, and served at No 4 Base Hospital, France.

READING George

RUSHTON J or T
Private   3rd Coldstream Guards

 Enlisted from Kineton House before 8/1/15. Listed as a casualty in May 1916.

SHEPHERD Joseph

SHEPHERD William
Born: 4/11/1887 (Bapt), Kineton

SHORTHALL James

SIMMONDS David J
Sergeant   Ox and Bucks L I
Enlisted: in September 1914.

 Wounded and was buried three times in eight hours.

SMITH Albert
Born: 21/5/1899, Kineton

Pronounced medically unfit and discharged in September 1917.

SMITH Ernest
Born: 19/2/1895 (Bapt), Kineton

SMITH Frank

SMITH Herbert Edwin
Corporal
Born: 21/9/88 (Bapt), Kineton   *Died:* 02/09/60, Kineton
Enlisted: Pre 23/11/17

SMITH William Henry
Private   Royal Army Medical Corps
Born: 24/12/1882 (Bapt), Kineton   *School:* Kineton
Enlisted: Pre May 1915

SMITH William Walter
Private Royal Army Medical Corps
Born: 18/12/1892 (Bapt), Kineton.   *School:* Kineton
Enlisted: Pre May 1915

Son of Walter Smith of Banbury Street, he was first home on leave in November 1917, after 2^1/$_2$ years in France

STANTON G
Enlisted: Pre 8/1/15

STREET Charles

STURDY C R
Private   9th Royal Warwickshire   201958

STURDY H

STURDY Mark W
Trooper   1st Warwickshire Yeomanry   310804

Invalided out of the Regiment on 7 December 1915, but rejoined, from Military Hospital, four months later. He received his wounds fighting against the Senussi in the Western Desert.

SUMNER Alfred Ernest

Born: 17/8/1890 (Bapt), Kineton

A horseman and labourer who lived in Mill Lane, Kineton, though employed by John Duckett in Chadshunt. He applied for exemption on the grounds that he was the only farm worker left on a farm previously employing six men, and was responsible for ploughing "four horse" land alone. His case was dismissed after appeal in April 1916, as it was felt that Mr Duckett could find annual labour if necessary.

SUMNER George

Private Royal Field Artillery

Born: 1890, Kineton   *School:* Kineton

Enlisted: Pre May 1915

SUMNER Percy Robert

Reginald   Royal Artillery

Born: 6/6/1890 (Bapt), Kineton   *School:* Kineton

Enlisted: Pre May 1915

SUMNER William James

Born: 23/2/1879 (Bapt), Kineton

Applied for exemption in March 1916. Living with his widowed mother in Southam Street, he was a bricklayer employed by Lord Willoughby de Broke. His application was refused, despite an appeal which described his mother as having a very bad leg which confined her to the house, and the statement that his younger brother had already enlisted.

SUTCLIFFE Newton

SUTCLIFFE Reginald

TALBOT Frederick
Sergeant Major   Canadian Force
School: Kineton   *Enlisted:* Pre May 1915

TALBOT Joseph
Born: 13/4/1888 (Bapt), Kineton

TALBOT Wallace

TAYLOR Albert George
Private   Ox and Bucks L I
Born: 30/3/1884 (Bapt), Kineton   *School:* Kineton
Enlisted: Pre May 1915

TAYLOR Ernest
Driver
School: Kineton   *Enlisted:* September 1914

TAYLOR Harry
Driver   Royal Field Artillery
School: Kineton   *Enlisted:* Pre May 1915

TAYLOR Lewis Walter
Private   Royal Field Artillery
Born: 30/12/1888 (Bapt), Kineton   *Enlisted:* Pre 7/9/17

TAYLOR R W

TIDMARSH Edward

TOWNSEND Fred
Rangers, London Company
Born: 22/3/1882 (Bapt), Kineton   *School:* Kineton
Enlisted: Pre May 1915

TRENFIELD Charles Henry MM
2nd Lieut   6th Dragoon Guards
Born: 23/7/1886 (Bapt), Kineton   *Enlisted:* December 1914.

Served in the London Regiment, and in the Warwickshire Yeomanry, before receiving a commission in the Dragoon Guards.

TRENFIELD Ernest G MSM
Private   Warwickshire Yeomanry
Born: 17/11/1891 (Bapt), Kineton   *School:* Kineton
Enlisted: Pre May 1915

TRENFIELD Richard
6th Royal Warwickshire
Born: 5/7/1891 (Bapt), Kineton   *School:* Kineton
Enlisted: Pre May 1915

TRITTON Lewis

Nephew of Lord Willoughby de Broke, living at the time of the outbreak of war with his aunt, the Hon Mabel Verney. Born 11 March 1879, married Kathleen Vere in 1924

TRITTON Oswald
Captain   Royal Artillery

Nephew of Lord Willoughby de Broke, living at the time of the outbreak of war with his Aunt, the Hon Mabel Verney. Born 28 July 1875, married Violet Margaret Sedgewick of Sherborne in August 1914. He died in 1963.

URWIN Albert Thomson
2nd Lieut   8th London (Post Office Rifles)
Born: 12/10/1890 (Bapt), Kineton   *School:* Kineton
Enlisted: Pre May 1915

URWIN Charles Robert
Born: 26/12/1883 (Bapt), Kineton

URWIN Walter Reginald
Corporal   Royal Air Force, 42nd squadron, HQ flight.
Born: 31/8/1888 (Bapt), Kineton

VERNEY Hon John Peyto MC
2nd Lieut   3rd Dragoons
Born: 25/5/1896   *Died:* 25/5/1986

The only son of Lord Willoughby de Broke. Inherited the title at the death of his father in 1923. Joined up on 14 August 1914, and almost immediately gazetted 2nd lieutenant in the 17th (Duke Of Cambridge's Own) Lancers transferring to the 3rd Dragoons in October 1914. Wounded in April 1918, after taking part in intense fighting for which he was awarded the Military Cross. After the war he became A.D.C. to the Governor of Bombay (1919 -1922), married in 1933, served with the Air Force at the Air Ministry in the Second World War, and settled in Kineton.

VERNEY Reynall
Royal Flying Corps
Born: 12/1/1886   *Died:* 27/10/1974

Nephew of Lord Willoughby de Broke. After service in the Flying Corps, stayed in the Royal Air Force, eventually becoming an Air Commodore. After the Second World War, and service with the Government of India, he returned to Warwickshire, became deputy Lieutenant of the county and churchwarden at Lighthorne parish church (1957-1966), where he died on 27 October 1974.

VICKERMAN H Frederick D
Captain   Royal Warwickshire

Enlisted in August 1914, and taken prisoner of war in February 1917

WATTS Edgar
Chauffeur to Mrs Falke of Green Cottage, he had four brothers in the Army, and consequently was eligible for exemption, for which he applied in May 1916. He was granted a month's exemption, but there is no record of any other appearances before the board, and presumably he enlisted at that time.

WEBB Ernest
Private   1st Herefordshire
School: Kineton   *Enlisted:* Pre May 1915

WELCH James

Applied for exemption in May 1916, and again a year later. Joshua Fielden supported his claim on the grounds that he was an expert horse-breeder and that it was felt necessary to keep a good horse stock with so many horses going to the front. His exemption was granted to avoid breaking up 'such a fine pack as the Warwickshire's', but it would appear that he signed up none-the-less.

WHEILDON Richard
Grenadier Guards

WILKINS Tom
Driver   Army Service Corps
Born: 9/5/1884 (Bapt), Kineton
Enlisted: 09/01/15, and served in Egypt.

WILKINS William Ernest
Born: 2/5/1897 (Bapt), Kineton

WILLOUGHBY DE BROKE Richard Greville, 19th Baron
Warwickshire Yeomanry

Rejoined the Warwickshire Yeomanry with the rank of Major on 1 September 1914. commanding 'B' squadron. Promoted Lieutenant Colonel of the Reserve Regiment on 7 January 1916.

WILLS Horace

WILLS John William Victor
Born: 9/7/1897 (Bapt), Kineton   *Died:* 02/10/69, Kineton

WILSON Walter
Royal Navy
   Brother of Arthur Wilson. See p 99

WISDOM Harry
Lance corporal   DCM   Rifle Brigade
Born: 25/3/1894 (Bapt), Kineton   *School:* Kineton
Enlisted: Pre May 1915   *Died:* 18/10/62, Kineton

WISDOM Martin
Sergeant   Royal Engineers
Born: 28/9/1883 (Bapt), Kineton   *Died:* 01/01/51, Kineton

WORRALL Thomas
Private Royal Artillery
Born: 19/5/1882 (Bapt), Kineton   *Died:* 16/8/1954, Kineton

WORRALL Thomas Eli
Born: 1888   *Died:* 28/06/1966, Kineton

YERBURGH Arthur Wardell
Born: 1891
A cousin of the Vicar, W H B Yerburgh

YERBURGH William Higgin Beauchamp
Chaplain   Royal Navy
Born: 19/8/1881   *Died:* 03/06/37, Bredon

Chapter Nine
The Hospital

Data about the VAD Hospitals all from *British Red Cross Society Annual Reports.*

Red Cross Hospitals in Warwickshire.(from *Warwickshire Branch Report*, 1917. page 12)

	No of Beds, April		
	1915	1916	1917
Brailes	10	10	12
Kineton	35	35	104
Solihull	25	37	106
Henley-in-Arden	30	30	70
Shipston-on-Stour	20	20	50
Hampton-in-Arden	40	40	100
Barford Hill, Warwick	20	32	40
Hill Crest, Coventry	30	40	53
Ashlawn, Rugby	45	—	—
Holmdene, Leamington	20	25	35
The Warren, Leamington	36	40	60
Olton	20	20	31
Kenilworth	34	34	50
Whytegates, Stratford-on-Avon		36	36
Guy's Cliffe, Warwick		24	35
St. Gerard's, Coleshill		40	50
Halloughton Hall, Coleshill		21	—
Clopton War Hospital, Stratford-on-Avon		106	106
Berkswell Rectory		20	22
Coleshill Vicarage, Coleshill		22	52
Hill House, Warwick		40	104
Marston Green		30	45
Pailton House, Rugby		30	33
Rugby Te Hera		20	40
Newnham Paddox		30	80

	No of Beds, April		
	1915	1916	1917
Springfield House, Knowle			28
Longfield, Sutton Coldfield			40
Weddington Hall, Nuneaton			60
Bilton hall, Rugby			55
Alcester			20
Halford Manor, Shipston-on-Stour			20
Rugby Infirmary			80
Southam			53
St. Bernard's, Sutton Coldfield			40
St. John's, Rugby			50
Maxstoke Castle, Coleshill			30
Farnborough Hall, Banbury			36
Totals	365	782	1826

The Hospital

Clarendon House V.A. Hospital : Staff 1915-1918

Opened : November 11th, 1914   Closed : December 21st, 1918

V.A.D.'s Warwick/8, Warwick/28, and Warwick/3

Commandants :
The Lady Willoughby de Broke Mrs D Fielden

Lady Superintendants :
Mrs Elkington (Trained nurse) Mrs J Griffin (Trained nurse)

Quarter-Masters :
The Hon. Mabel Verney Mrs M Pierson-Webber

*Assistant Quarter-Master:*The Lady Willoughby
Mrs Woodfield

Pharmacist :
Mr Beeby

Medical Officers :
Lloyd J H Oldmeadow, MD., FRCS (Edinburgh)
Frederick V Elkington, LRCS (Edinburgh), LRCP

Trained Nurses :
Sister Thomlinson   Sister Nisbett

Staff and Helpers :

Abbott, Mr Henry	Bancroft, Mr Geoffrey	Blunt, Mr Robert
Alcock, Miss Maud	Bancroft, Mrs Florence	Boulton , Miss Kathleen
Aldridge, Miss Clara	Barlow, Miss M	Boulton, Mrs Mary
Alexander, Mrs Caroline	Barnes, Miss Sarah	Bran, Miss Mary
Allibone, Junior, Mrs	Batchelor, Mrs Marion	Briscoe, Mrs
Allibone, Senior, Mrs	Batchelor, Mrs Sarah	Buckmaster, Mrs
Anderson, Mrs Lorna	Bates, Mrs	Burnham, Mrs Florence
Atkinson, Mrs Janet	Beeby, Mr Robert	Burton, Mr Alfred
Baldwin, Mr Arthur	Bennett, Mrs Edith	Bush, Miss Cicely
Baldwin, Mrs Mary J	Berridge, Mrs	Carter, Miss Mary (Cook)

Cartwright, Mrs Susan
Chandler, Miss Rose
Chandler, Mrs Bessie
Chappell, Mrs Christine
Charlton, Miss Violet
Chenevix Trench, Miss Doris
Clarke, Mrs
Clarke, Mrs James
Clerk, Miss B
Clerk, Miss Mary
Clerk, Miss Valmia
Collett, Miss Daisy
Collins, Miss Elsie
Collins, Mrs
Collins, Mrs Walter
Cooper, Miss May
Cooper, Mrs Elizabeth
Corbally, Mrs
Court, Miss Mary L
Crawford-Wood, Miss
Crossley, Mrs J B
Crossley, Mrs Janet
Davies, Miss
Dixon, Miss (Cook)
Dodd, Miss Hilda
Dodd, Miss May
Doyle, Miss Mary
Duckett, Miss Ethel
Dummelow, Mrs Cicely
Dunn, Mrs
Durham, Mr David
Dyer, Mrs
Edkins, Mrs Mary
Edwards, Miss Gwendoline
Elkington, Miss Evelyn
Ellis Mrs Sarah
Elong, Miss Clara
Fairfax, Miss Phyllis
Fessey, Miss Elizabeth

Fielden, Mrs
Fisher, Miss Helen
Fisher, Mr Jack
Fitch, Miss Dulce
Ford, Mrs
Francis, Miss Winifred
Freeman, Miss May
Freeman, Mr Harry W
Garrard, Miss Marjorie
Garrard, Mrs Marion
Garrett, Miss May
Garrett, Mr James
Gaskell, Miss Brenda
Gaskell, Miss Joyce
Gaskell, Miss Nancy
Gaskell, Mrs
Gilks, Miss Alice
Golder, Miss Mildred
Gore, Mrs Harriet
Grant, Miss Edna
Greenslade, Mrs
Griffin, Miss Mary
Griffin, Miss Sarah
Griffin, Mrs M E
Groom, Miss Ethel
Hamilton, Mrs
Hanbury, Hon Mrs Patience
Hancock, Miss May
Hardy, Miss Gladys
Harris, Miss Maggie
Harrison, Miss Bleney
Hartwell, Miss Annie
Heath-Stubbs, Miss Alice
Heath-Stubbs, Miss Lily
Heath-Stubbs, Mr Frank
Herring, Mrs
Hillier, Miss
Holbech, Miss Marjorie
Holbech, Miss Olive

Holbech, Mrs Catherine
Holder, Miss Elsie
Howell, Mrs Elizabeth
Howes, Miss May
Humphriss, Mrs
Hunter, Miss Joyce
Hunter, Miss Mary
Hurst, Miss
Hutchinson, Miss (Sister)
Hutton, Miss Marjorie
Hutton, Miss Nellie
Isfield, Miss Mabel
Johnson, Miss Florence
Jones, Miss Joan
Joslyn, Mrs Lizzie (Cook)
Keech, Miss Lilian
Kemp-Welch, Mrs Marion
Kerrison, Miss Betty
Lakin, Mrs Sybil
Lansbury, Miss Ethel
Leaf, Mrs
Lindsey, Miss
Liveing, Miss Catherine
Liveing, Miss Marjorie
Long, Miss May
MacDougall, Miss Minnie
MacNicol, Miss
Martin, Miss Florence
Maurice, Miss Gladys
McCullock, Mrs Catherine
Meyrick, Miss Cicely
Miller, Miss F
Mills, Miss Phoebe
Mills, Mrs Frances
Mizen, Mrs
Montgomery, Miss Winsome
Moore, Miss May
Motion, Miss Kathleen
Mullis, Mrs Alice

Naylor, Mr J
Nesbitt, Miss (Sister)
Newbold, Mr J
Oldmeadow, Miss Ruth
Oldmeadow, Mrs
Padbury, Mr William
Page, Miss Daisy Maria
Perdue, Miss
Perry, Miss Pauline
Perry, Mr D
Pett, Miss Amy Maria
Pierson-Webber, Miss Margery
Porter, Miss Annie
Potter, Miss Florence
Prater, Miss Constance
Pratt, Mrs
Price, Miss Jane
Price, Mrs (Cook)
Pullen, Mr J
Rawlins, Mr William
Rogerson, Miss Florence
Russell, Miss (Sister)
Salmon, Miss Alice
Sandback, Miss Hester

Seagur, Mrs
Seaton, Miss (Cook)
Shand, Miss Sylvia
Sharples, Miss
Smith, Miss Dorothy
Smith, Miss Ethel
Smith, Miss Gladys
Smith, Mrs Lucy
Smith-Barry, Mrs
Spencer, Miss Auriel
Spencer, Miss Emily
Spencer, Miss Lizzie
Stanley, Mrs Gladys
Stock, Mrs
Styles Mrs
Styles, Miss Agnes
Styles, Mr George
Sumner, Mr F G
Taylor, Miss
Thomlinson, Miss (Sister)
Tiley, Miss Alice Orme
Tiley, Mr George Orme
Todd, Miss Penelope
Trenfield, Miss Lilian

Tweed, Mr A
Tyrrwhitt-Drake, Mrs Margery
Verney, Hon Mabel
Verney, Miss Clare
Wade, Mrs May
Waldron, Mrs L Constance
Walker, Mr Thomas
Walters, Miss Ellen
Waterman, Mrs
Wattam, Mrs
Weatherby, Mrs Eva
Webb, Miss Minnie
Webb, Mr Guernsey
Weir, Miss
Wells, Mrs Jean
Wheildon, Miss Olive
Williams, Miss Dorothy
Williams, Mrs Agatha
Willock, Miss Lois
Wincott, Miss May
Woodfield, Mrs Ada
Yerburgh, Miss O
Yerburgh, Rev W H B
Young, Miss G

Chapter Ten
Brief Biographies of Some Village Leaders

The Verney Family
Richard Greville Verney,
19th Baron, Lord Willoughby de Broke, 1869-1923
Marie Frances Lisette, Lady Willoughby de Broke, 1868-1941

The Willoughby de Broke family had been Lords of the Manor of Kineton since they acquired the title in 1806 from the Earl of Warwick, and of Little Kineton since 1823.

As Lords of the Manor they were expected to lead village activities, and, until the end of the war, in many ways they still played the part of feudal lords - for example, owning much of the village land and property, and expecting to care for their tenants in times of sickness and difficulty. Thus it is not surprising that Lord Willoughby de Broke was instrumental in setting up the Volunteer Training Corps, and in organising the War Memorial appeal, nor that his wife should be closely involved in the Clarendon House V A Hospital.

Aged 45 years at the outbreak of the war, Richard Greville Verney had been Conservative member for the Rugby division of Warwickshire from 1895 to 1900. Like his father and grandfather before him, he was Master of the Warwickshire Hunt, and was well known for outspoken views on foxhunting, (writing *Hunting the Fox*, and *The Sport of Our Ancestors*) as well as for his stand in the Lords against Liberal proposals for the reform of the Lords. At the outbreak of war he held over 6000 acres around Kineton and in Northamptonshire, and lived at Compton Verney, the family seat about two miles north of Kineton, and at Woodley House, now Haven House rest home for the elderly, which became his principal residence in 1920.

In 1895 he married Marie Frances Lisette Hanbury, youngest daughter of Charles Hanbury of Strathgarve, Ross-shire. Just as her husband's interests lay mainly with the hunt and in politics, so his wife was known as a fine horsewoman, and for her clear political views. She was extremely interested in Women's Suffrage, and was an active President for Warwickshire of the

Richard Greville Verney, 19th Lord Willoughby de Broke

Conservative and Unionist Franchise Association. For her work at Clarendon hospital she was awarded the OBE, but after her husband died in 1923, increasingly poor health forced her to winter in Egypt, until she died at the age of 73.

At the death of her husband, their only son, John Peyto Verney, inherited the title.

John Peyto Verney, 1896-1986, their only son.

Educated at Eton and Sandhurst, John Peyto Verney was aged 18 at the beginning of the war. He inherited the title of 20th Lord Willoughby de Broke in 1923, and ten years later married Rachel Wrey. He continued to live in Kineton for most of the rest of his life, first at Woodley House and later at Fox Cottage, off the Market Square.

After his military career in World War One, John Peyto maintained a lifelong interest in aviation, and was the owner of a private airstrip in Kineton (just to the south of the Gaydon Road before reaching Chadshunt). He was at the Air Ministry during World War Two. He became Lord Lieutenant of Warwickshire from 1939 until 1967. He devoted most of his life to the Turf but he was also landlord of St Martin's Theatre, London. The theatre had been built by his father in 1916, and in 1961 he spent £40,000 on its restoration, in a venture which he declared was "more risky than the Turf". This expenditure was no doubt enabled by the sale of 4000 acres of land in 1957. By the time of his death, although the family still owned some farms and land, much of the estate had gone, the Kineton house had been sold, and Compton Verney had changed hands many times and was almost derelict.

The Honourable Mabel Verney, 1855-1937

Aunt of the 19th Lord Willoughby de Broke.

Mabel Verney had already attained 'retirement' age at the time of the outbreak of war. Throughout her life she had played a large part in village affairs, particularly as representative of the Parish on the Stratford Board of Guardians, which she joined in 1894, and later the Rural District Council. She was co-opted on to Warwickshire Education Committee, where she became well known for her spirited defence of small rural schools, and was keenly interested in a project to build a church senior school in Kineton. During the Great War she served in the VAD hospital. Her interest in the Red Cross continued, and she was deeply involved with the Kineton and District Nursing Association.

She lived in Kineton all her life, first at Diana Lodge, Little Kineton, and later at The Craddocks, now Heronwood House, Banbury Street. She died in 1937, at the age of 81 years, and is buried by the south wall of the parish church.

The Hon Patience Hanbury, 1873-1965

Sister of the 19th Lord Willoughby de Broke, and consequently niece of the Hon. Mabel Verney, Patience Hanbury was one of those who stayed in Kineton, and like her aunt, was a well-known Kineton resident for many years.

Patience was born at Compton Verney, at a time when the house was in its heyday, and when her father owned some 18000 acres of land and was the patron of nine livings. In 1896 she married Basil Hanbury, third son of Charles Hanbury. She campaigned vigorously for both the Suffragist Movement and for the Conservative Party, and was honoured with a long service medal for her support of the Soldiers' Sailors' and Airmen's Families' Association, a charity with which she was closely involved as area organiser in the days of the Great War. Within Kineton she was Secretary of the Kineton and District Nursing Association until its amalgamation with the National Health Service in 1947. As well as the interest in hunting which led her to become the Warwickshire Hunt correspondent of the Horse and Hound, she also was passionately interested in village cricket, and wrote a small book about the history of Kineton Cricket Club.

She died in Kineton at the age of ninety-two.

The Fielden family

Joshua Fielden, 1866-1944

Joint Master of the Fitzwilliam Hunt (Peterborough area), from 1892 to 1895, Joshua Fielden came to Kineton in 1911 as joint master of the Warwickshire after a short time in Farnborough. At the time he came to Kineton, he was described as a man who

> *is a real master of fox-hunting. He treats it as an art, and might almost be said to live for nothing else. Withal he is a particularly fine horseman, riding the biggest best-bred horses that can be bought. He is very cool, has a fine eye for a country, and knows all the time what the hounds are doing.*[1]

Perhaps Mabel Verney's comment at the end of the War- that "he had to find consolation by working in the kennels from morning to night" had not been the hardship one imagines!

He and his wife, Dora, lived at Kineton House, which later became Norton Approved School. It is now split into private apartments, and is once again called the Mansion House, as it was in the nineteenth century when it was the home of Georgiana, dowager Lady Willoughby de Broke. During the whole of the Fielden's time there, both during and after the war, Kineton

Joshua Fielden, Joint Master of Foxhounds

House and its beautiful grounds seem to have been the centre of almost every fete and 'treat' for school children. There they were entertained to "Punch and Judy", sports and enormous teas. At other times, large houseparties were held for the Fielden's hunting friends and for their eligible young daughter, Joan. Joshua Fielden's first wife, Marion, was the eldest daughter of Colonel Sir Edward Sladen. She never came to Kineton, but bore him his only son, Lionel, who was aged twenty at the outbreak of War, and is named on Kineton's Roll of Honour. Joan, on the other hand, came to Kineton at the age of five and was brought up at Kineton House. The family's love of horses was inherited by this only daughter. Joan married Mr Douglas Forster at St Margaret's, Westminster, in 1932, and her son, Captain Timothy Forster, is a well known Racing Trainer.

Joshua died in 1944, and is buried in Burton Dassett churchyard.

Dora Fielden, 1871-1953

Dora Fielden is the major exception to the observation that Kineton lost its leaders soon after the war. Her leadership of the community had only just begun. She was the third daughter of Mr. Thomas Henry Ismay, of Dawpool, Merseyside, owner of the White Star Shipping Line. She married Joshua

Fielden in 1901, and came to Kineton with him in 1911. She immediately began to interest herself in the welfare of the village, helped found the Women's Institute, and was its president for most of thirty-eight years. It was through her influence that the former Women's Institute Hall was built, on the site where the present village hall now stands.

She shared her husband's enthusiasm for the hunt, and was a keen follower of the hounds for many years. During the First World War, she was Commandant of the V.A.D. Hospitals in Kineton House, Clarendon House and Walton House. It was for her magnificent work during this period that she was awarded the O.B.E.

Her contribution over many years to public life in the village and at county level was immense.

Red Cross Association:	County Director and Vice-President.
Land Army :	County Chairman (World War Two)
Women's Voluntary Service:	Centre Leader (Stratford area)
Women's Institute :	Warwickshire Federation Executive Committee, and President 1933 President, Kineton, much of 1917-1954
Rural District Council:	Kineton representative for twelve years
Board of Guardians:	Member
Kineton Nursing Association	Chairman and Treasurer
Conservative Association, Kineton branch	Treasurer
Girl guides' Association	President
School Manager	

She died in December 1953 at her sister's London home and was buried beside her husband at Burton Dassett church at a simple family ceremony.

Captain Anthony Fielden 1886-1972

Nephew of Joshua and Dora Fielden.

Aged 28 at the outbreak of war, Captain Anthony married Phoebe Brand at the end of July 1914. He and his wife spent their first years together, when he was on leave, at the Manor House, home of Phoebe's mother, and at the end of the War he bought Clarendon House, though it is doubtful whether they lived there for long.

He ended the war as a Major, and later attained the rank of Lieutenant Colonel. In 1925 he was Master of Foxhounds to the South Salop Hounds, and from 1929-1932 to the North Cotswold pack. In 1954 he became High Sheriff of Shropshire, and he died at his Ludlow home in 1972.

The Vicars of Kineton

1912-1920 William Higgin Beauchamp Yerburgh

The vicar of St Peter's at the time of the war was William Yerburgh. He came to the parish in 1912, at the age of 31 years. In 1915 he was seriously ill, and absent from duties for some months. The nature of his illness is not known, but it involved a long spell of recuperation in Brighton. Nevertheless, despite interruptions of illness, and his war service, he achieved a lot in terms of church and vicarage maintenance, in particular the restoration of the bells and belfry, and was a powerful and charismatic preacher.

William Yerburgh returned to Kineton after his war service for only a very brief period before exchanging parishes with Hugh Holbech, and thus becoming Rector of St Giles, Bredon, Worcestershire in 1920. He married Frances Sylvia Whitmore in Tewkesbury abbey in 1925. He died in Bredon.

1920-1934 Hugh Holbech

The successor to William Yerburgh was a local man. Born in 1859, Hugh Holbech succeeded his father as Rector of Farnborough in June 1896. From 1911 until 1920 he was rector of Bredon, Worcestershire, but, a hunting man, he was a close friend of the 19th Lord Willoughby de Broke, and took the living at Kineton in 1920, just before the death of that lord, exchanging parishes with William Yerburgh. The living was amalgamated with that of Combroke in 1926, by which time he had become a Canon of Coventry Cathedral. He retired to Farnborough in 1934, and died at there, at his family home, in December, 1949, at the age of ninety-two.

Hugh Holbech

1890-1894 Arthur Hawtrey Watson

The Rector of Lighthorne and Vicar of Chesterton, two neighbouring parishes, continued to be another well-known Kineton figure. Arthur Watson had been a young man when he came to Kineton at the age of twenty-five, from being a curate near Slough. Almost straightaway he had gas put in the church to enable him to hold evening services instead of the afternoon services which had been customary until then. He appointed Mr. G. W. Webb as organist and choirmaster, and a surpliced choir began to sit in the chancel, whereas previously there had been only a small choir in the gallery.

After only four years in Kineton he moved several times before returning to become Rector of Lighthorne in 1908, and did not leave there until 1936. He died in 1952 in Norfolk at the age of eighty-seven, but is buried in Lighthorne, close to the War Memorial.

Arthur Watson

1894-1912 Leonard Edward William Victor Goodenough

Predecessor to William Yerburgh was Leonard Goodenough who had been vicar in Kineton for eighteen years. He was well known for his love of good music, and was responsible for the installation of the present organ casing, reredos and screen in St Peter's Church, Kineton. (The organ was placed in the church in 1896 in memory of the Lady Geraldine Willoughby de Broke.)

During the War he was chaplain to the Warwickshire Yeomanry both in England and in Egypt, and later in the war was an interpreter to the British

Military Mission in Rome, and secretary at the Versailles Peace Conference. He died in 1920 at his parish near Sittingbourne, Kent, at the age of fifty-five years, but his long association with Kineton was remembered by his brother Vice Admiral Sir William Goodenough KCB, who presented Kineton parish church with an ancient Italian processional cross in his memory.

Leonard Goodenough

The Schoolmasters
Guernsey Walsingham Webb 1866-1940

Throughout the first World War, and indeed for some years before it, one of the most influential figures, and seemingly a man of boundless energy, was Guernsey Walsingham Webb.

For someone rejoicing in such a name, it is surprising that he was the son of an Independent minister, born in Stroud and brought up not far from

Bristol, and seems to have no connection with Norfolk, or indeed with High Church. The first reference to him being in Kineton is as teacher at a school for "young gentlemen" at Clarendon House, at a time when his sister ran a school for "young ladies" at the same address. In 1889 he became Headmaster of the "Middle Class School" in Warwick Road, a school founded in about 1862 by Lady Willoughby de Broke as a boy's boarding school, which lasted at the same address until the middle of the 1920's.

The school, under his leadership, seems to have been extremely successful, but he may be best remembered for his contribution to the musical life of the village, being made organist and choirmaster at St Peter's church in 1890 (appointed by Arthur Watson), a founder of the Choral Society, and organiser of innumerable concerts. He was churchwarden from 1912 until 1923. Not content with organising the musical life of Kineton, in 1907 he became conductor of the Stratford-upon-Avon Choral Society, a position which he held until 1920. He was much praised for his conducting "with no fancy beating, a good straight down, across, up, beat, with a definite bringing in of the various parts, so that the chorus could never be in doubt...."[2] At the time that the Stratford Herald was singing his praises, not only was Major Bairnsfather the conductor of the Orchestral section, but Marie Corelli, the Stratford novelist and conservationist was a regular attender, and on several occasions expressed her thanks personally to Mr Webb, and made generous money donations to the Stratford choir.[3]

He married in 1919, and was ordained after a period of study at Wycliffe Hall, Oxford in 1923 at the age of fifty seven. He left Kineton to become curate to William Yerburgh at Bredon for a short time, running the church at Bredon's Norton, and, of course, building up this church choir to customary heights, before, in 1926, becoming Vicar of Longdon, Tewkesbury, Gloucestershire. He died there in 1940.

Joseph Chandler, c.1863-1930

Another war time leader was Joseph Chandler, Headmaster of the National school from 1884-1923

Joseph Chandler was a popular school master and member of the community, who seems to have fulfilled the desire of his mother to "be obliging" - her words to him when he left his Sussex home to come to Kineton in 1884. In nearly every school photograph he appears with either his violin or his penny- whistle, and he also played the organ. During his

Joseph Chandler, with his violin and surrounded by school children on May Day

years in Kineton he saw teacher's salaries rise from a pittance to what he, at least, saw as an acceptable level, great developments in curriculum, and the school leaving age rise from eleven to fourteen. As well as running the school he was expected to teach a class of forty or fifty children.

Within a year of arriving in the village, Joseph Chandler was secretary of the Horticultural Society, and continued to be active in the public life of the village from then on, for example as Secretary of the Gas Company, in connection with War Savings, as Sunday School Superintendent, in support of the Street Lighting scheme, and many ways.

At his retirement from the school he was presented with an excellent gold hunter watch, with double gold chain as a token of the high esteem with which he was held in the village.

The Agent
William Webb Hutton 1862-1930

William Hutton lived on the estates of the Lords Willoughby de Broke all his life, for his father was agent for 30 years. He took over duties from Mr

Squarey when he himself became agent to the Warwickshire and Northamptonshire estates of Lord Willoughby de Broke in July 1903. He married a resident of Benifield, Northamptonshire, and his familiarity with that area may explain why Kineton's War Memorial is based so closely on the cross at Brigstock.

He was made People's Warden at St Peter's Church in 1915, and remained Churchwarden until his death in 1930 at the age of sixty-eight.

The Doctor
Doctor Lloyd John Hollis Oldmeadow

Born in 1871 in Hobart, Tasmania, Dr Oldmeadow came to Kineton following in the family tradition of being a doctor, as medical officer and public vaccinator. At first he lived at, and practised from, "North Lodge" (now the library), the fifth General Practioner to work from that address. He later lived at Fighting House, the old house in Fighting Close. At the end of his military career he became involved with the VAD Hospital in Kineton

1 *Stratford upon Avon Herald*, 20 January, 1911
2 ibid., 10 December 1920
3 **Diana Brownhill.** *An Illustrated History of the Stratford upon Avon Choral Society.* 1982, p 66-69.

Index of Names

See also Chapters 8 and 9 for lists of soldiers and hospital staff.

Allsebrook, Mr. 10
Anderson, Miss M 38
Ashford, Mr. 11
Askew, Pte F 77
Askew, Pte G E 76
Askew, Pte H S 77
Askew, Pte O J. 77

Bairnsfather, Captain B. . . 36,37,38
Baldwin, Mrs M. 41
Bancroft, G 12
Barnes, Corporal W. 78-79
Bishop, W 30
Booth, J F & Son 55
Boulton, Miss K. 40
Brand, Mrs 5,7,32
Bretherick, W 12
Brigden, Rev T E 58
Brisker, Mr 52,60

Carrington Smith, Lt Col. 14
Carter, Miss 32,41
Chandler, J . . 11,13,33,47,51,142-3
Clifton, E 13,22
Coles,E 11
Collett, Lance Corpl J E W . . . 67-69
Coventry, Bishop of. 57,60
Cowley, J A. 69-70

Dalgety, Mrs 5
Day, Miss 10

Elkington, Dr 29,32,41
Ellick, C. 3

Fielden, J 9,11,17,18,21,22,27
36,58,60,135-6

Fielden, Mrs D . . . 5,6,12,13,18,27,
28,35,39,41,42,43,136-7
Fielden, Captain A 7,137-8
Fisher J. 11,50,52,60
Fisher, 2nd Lieut P W 79-80
Fisher, Captain R W 80-82
Fisher, J B 82
Flower, Mrs A D 9
Freeman, G 21
Freeman, H 12
Freeman, Mrs 41

Gage, General 58
Gardner, F. 27
Garland, Mr. 32
Garrett,Mr 33
Gaskell, Mrs. 5,32,48
Geden, Mr 52
Gilks, Mr. 51
Goodenough, Rev L V W. . . . 140-1
Goulder, Miss M. 41
Griffin, A 11,22
Griffin, F. 11
Griffin, J 60
Grimes, S 22

Hanbury, Col B. 11,12,43
Hanbury, The Hon Mrs P . . 12,13,47
52,134-5
Hancock, F 12
Heath Stubbs, Mr. 13
Heath Stubbs, Miss 13
Hiatt, Mrs 47
Hobbs, Mrs 10
Holbech, Rev H. 47,58,138-9
Holbech, Mrs M 41,47

Holbech, Miss M W 41
Hooten, Mr 52
Hunter, Miss 6
Hutton, Captain W H 3,70-73
Hutton, W W 10,50,143-4

Jickling, Rev C 45

Knight, Mr J. 53

Lakin, Mr 12
Lakin, Mrs. 41

Moore, Miss 41
Motion, A 32
Murray, The Hon Lady. 7

Napier, Brigadier General 14

Oldmeadow, Dr 11,19,24,41,48,144
Orme Tiley, Mr. 41

Parke, E. 13,30,38
Perry, Miss 12
Pierson Webber, Mrs 12,29
Potter, Miss 41
Price, Dr 29,36

Smith, Lieut D G. 82-3
Smith, Captain R F 83-4
Smith, Inspector. 11
Smith, Miss E 41
Smith, Miss G 41
Sumner, F G 6,21,48,52,60
Sumner, F S. 11
Sutcliffe, Mr 11

Thomas, Corporal H. 39
Thursby Pelham, J 24
Trenfield, 2nd Lieut C 75-76
Trenfield, Pte E 76
Trenfield, Pte R. 73-74
Trenfield, W 22,47
Tritton, Captain O 7

Verney, 2nd Lieut J P 7,133-4
Verney, H B. 13
Verney, R 13
Verney, Miss C. 13
Verney, The Hon M . . . 12,21,29,32
41,42,52,60,134

Wade, Miss M 41
Waldron, Mrs. 41
Watson, Rev A H 12,58,139
Webb Miss M 13,36
Webb, G W 2,5,13,29,36,41
43,58,141-2
Whately, Miss 6
Wheildon, S. 13
Williams, Pte F 30
Willock, Miss L 41
Willoughby de Broke, Lord . . 17,19
22,29,50,52,55,58,132-3
Willoughby de Broke, Lady . . 12,23
29,30,35,39,41,43,132-3
Wisdom, H 19,67
Woodfield, Mrs 41

Yerburgh, Rev W H B 12,47
58,64-7,138
Yerburgh, Miss 12,13